HOME ON THE HILL

W. D. Merchant

HOME ON THE HILL

A Bombay Girlhood

An Original by Three Continents Press
Washington, D.C.

Original First Edition by Three Continents Press
1901 Pennsylvania Avenue N.W.
Washington, D.C. 20006

Library of Congress Cataloging-in-Publication Data
Merchant, W. D., 1946-
Home on the hill: a Bombay girlhood / by W.D. Merchant. – 1st ed.
p. cm.
ISBN 0-89410-712-7 (alk. paper) : $20.00. – ISBN 0-89410-713-5 (pbk.: alk. paper) : 12.00
1. Merchant, W. D. 2. Parsees–India–Bombay–Biography.
3. Bombay (India)–Biography. I. Title
DS432.P3M47 1991
954'.7923'0099—dc 20
[B] 91-65184
CIP

for D. A. M.

Grateful acknowledgement is made for the use of two maps. That of Bombay & Environs is adapted from a map on p. 16 of the late Elsie V. Baptista's *The East Indians,* by courtesy of the Institute of Indian Culture, Bombay. The map of Mahabaleshwar Plateau comes from the 17th edn. of *Murray's Handbook for Travellers in India, Pakistan, Burma and Ceylon,* p. 356, by kind permission of the publisher, John Murray.

Contents

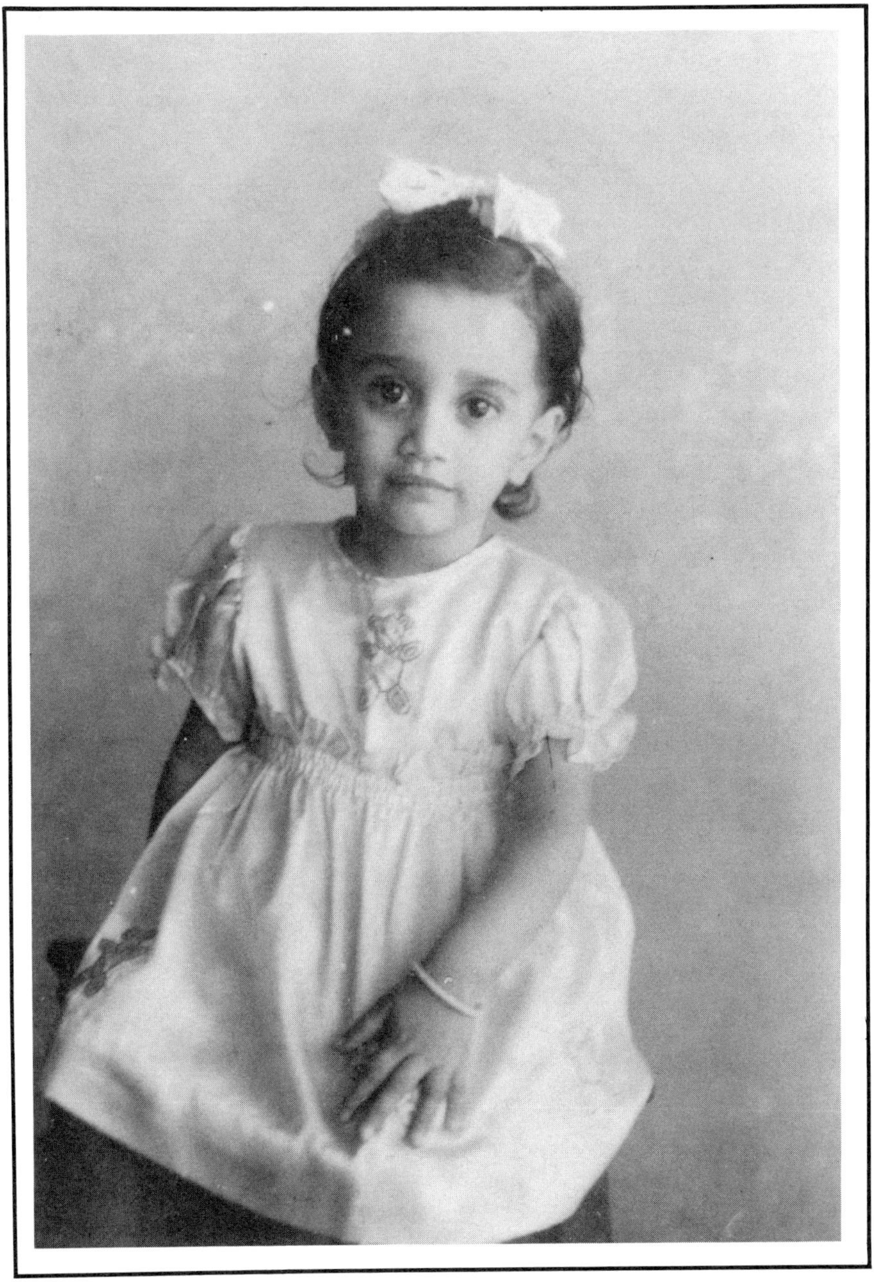

Myself at Two

Mother at Seventeen

My Sister, Aged Two, 1952

Mother and Her Three Children, 1950

My Brother and I, about 1948

My Mother at Mahabaleshwar, with the Youngest

Myself in Kindergarten

Visiting the Hill-Station Apiary

The Boarding School Visit

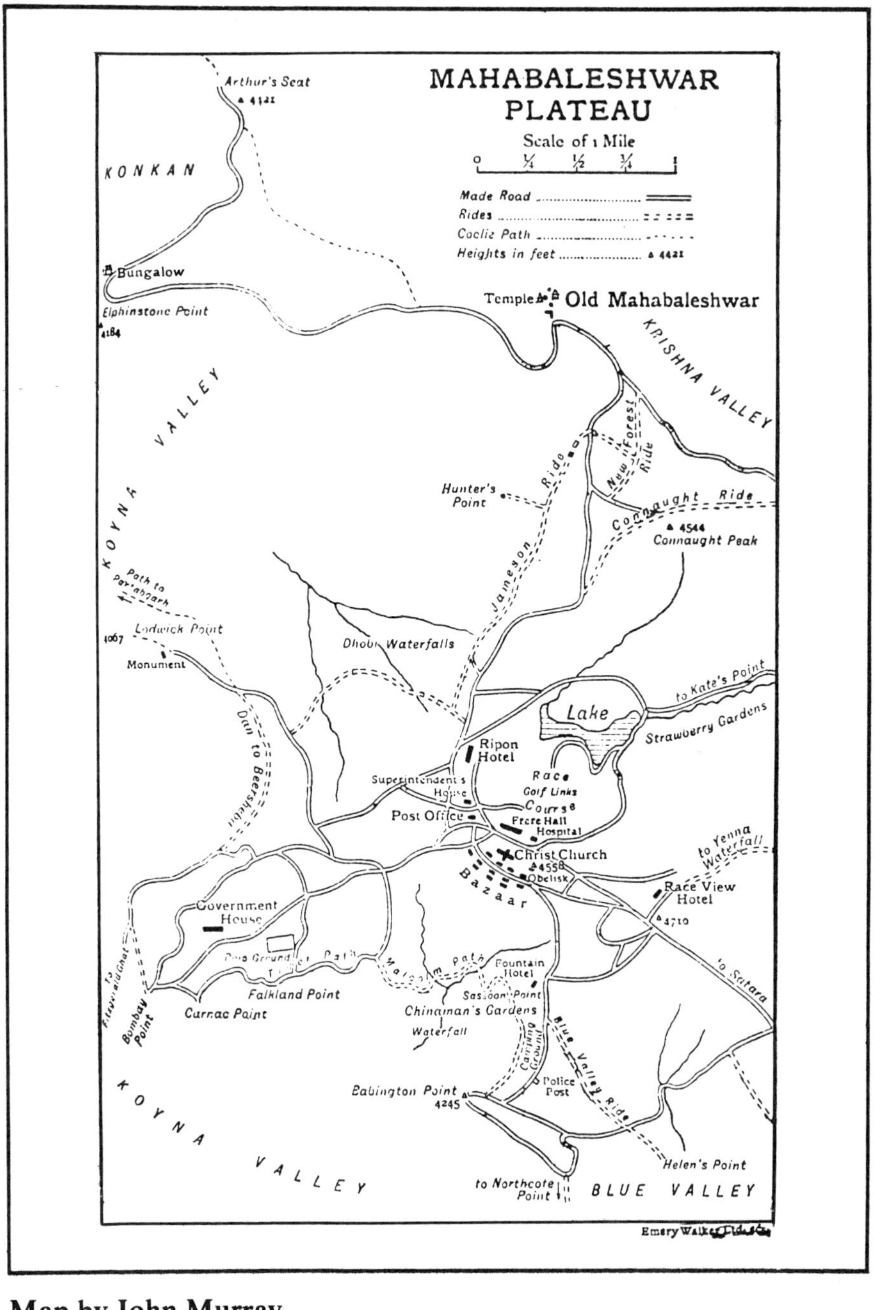

Map by John Murray

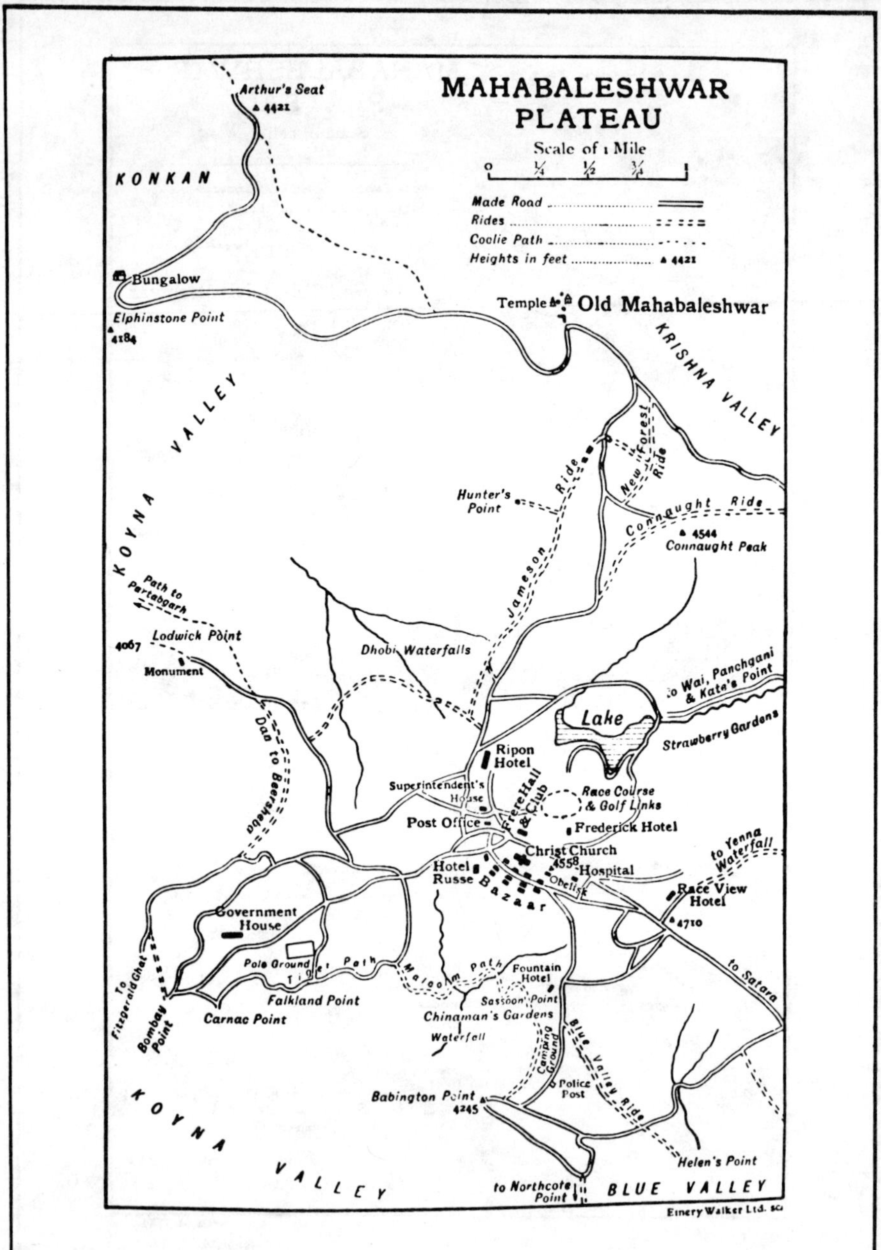

Map by John Murray

ONE

What sorrow has he who has
no family and no wealth?

— Tamil proverb

My brother writes poetry. He writes about the pain of being himself. I live in America, the land of the common man and of common sense. My brother is not common, that is why he lives on beaches in Greece and in the rubble of the West Bank.

I dreamt the first paragraph whole, in its entirety, as I waited to wake up to the strains of Mozart on my alarm. It is sunrise as I sit in my garden room. The tiled roof of the garage is powdered with snow from a late storm. It looks waffled, like the blistered pad I found beneath the carpet when I redid my floors. The buds on the magnolia are blackened by the unexpected cold. I'll miss their exuberant excess this year. A perfect red sun sits in the bare branches of the hawthorn turning to gold as it climbs the sky.

I had to learn the names of the trees when I got here. I grew up with jackfruit and mangoes and *koels* crying in rising crescendo in the lovingly planted English rose garden. I was amazed at how erect pine trees stand in straight rows like sentinels on Michigan highways, how little a juniper or a spruce bends. I long for the spreading banyan tree, so solid with its hanging roots seeking to return to earth. If Buddha had sat under one of these instead of a peepul, he would have understood the meaning of reality right away. Life itself is the meaning, to return to dust and come up again as a new branch.

Even my brother in his nihilist frenzies knows life. When among strangers, he throws himself into their history, makes their present his concern and weeps over their future in his poems. But then, even as a child, he was happiest being not himself. As I played choosy princess, he taped to his forearm all the ribbons he could find in the house and bits of golden string that came wrapped around baskets of summer fruits smelling of straw and the fragrance of Alfonso mangoes. He was the "ribbon-seller." He ran through inter-connecting rooms calling out his wares and I see him now, a whirl of streamers, in the still of a tropical afternoon. As the sheep trot past our place to the slaughterhouse raising puffs of dust and scenting the air with their damp wool, I stop the ribbon-seller's mad dash. I will buy his gaudy wares, perhaps the broad white one with blue polka-dots or the shiny pink satin one which only my fairer younger sisters got to wear, or perhaps the shot-silk one in iridescent shades of violet. He didn't really want to sell them, merely to argue with me about their quality and their price. If I bought one, the game would be over and he would have to be himself by himself.

I often banished him from my presence. I could not bear his uncomprehending hurt. He was always in trouble. At two he broke Father's commandment: Thou shalt not eat cookies in bed. When the commandment giver got home, half-inch long fire ants had made a nest among the crumbs in the bed sheets. In a rage at being disobeyed, he stripped my brother naked and planted him on top of that writhing mass. I ran out, breaking several commandments myself; out of the house, out of hearing of my brother's sobs, out of range of Father's rage and Mother's despair. I did not look at or speak to my father for three whole days.

I want to write about my father, but I can't find the right tone in which to speak of him. Mother said that as an infant I stood at the door for hours at a time when he left each morning. I still hate to see a man leave for any reason.

Each evening Father helped me pack my books for the coming day in a little blue briefcase. He read aloud the timetable, "geography, arithmetic, Gujarati," and I scrambled amidst all my books spread out on his bed picking the right ones to pack. We made a good team. I always knew what he needed, whether it was silence or a chance to be wise. At four I already knew when to ask him the right questions so he could teach me how to plot strategy whilst all the time talking of God's will and Fate's propensity to play Russian roulette with the best laid plans.

He was sentimental but hated displays of emotion unless they were negative. One could yell and beat up taxi drivers who cut into his lane in the traffic. But one could not show the slightest affection in public or private. He was mortified when I hugged him at the airport on a brief visit home from America. I don't remember either of my parents ever kissing me or even holding me on their lap, but I did get more than my share of verbal praise. "My lucky one," he called the middle child; "my wise one," he said with pride about me. He punished me very rarely and always for the same reason. I would not eat. The smell and sight of food nauseated me and even when I was ravenously hungry, I could not bear to ask for food. I fantasize about food, perfect dishes, perfectly served by perfectly trained servants, but real food does not appeal. It started perhaps with sudden vertigo from a wire fruit basket whose shadow moved back and forth over my plate like a giant spider's web as it swung freely in the breeze from the small kitchen window. I burst into tears from the giddiness. My father threatened to have a doctor inject egg yolks directly into my veins and when that brought on greater floods of tears, he beat me. My choking sobs made it impossible to swallow. Then he tried not letting me leave the table till I finished. The morning cup of milk was reheated and cooled several times as breakfast stretched into lunch.

Lunch was inedible from all the salt of my crying into it. At dinner I threw up. He let me off in disgust. Then he hit on a new way to get some nourishment into me. He put a drop of pure raspberry essence into a saucer of milk and I would have to drink it to reach the ruby red drop. I'd figure out the closest point on the rim of the saucer to the drop and drink from that side, so he started putting it in the dead center of the plate. I lost interest in that game very quickly.

He often told me how at the end of the war, with food scarce, he had walked miles and visited every dry goods store in the city to find English Peek-Frean biscuits because I had actually eaten a whole one enthusiastically.

In a starving land food is the central preoccupation. But Indians are ambiguous about food. Annapurna, the goddess of food, is an aspect of Kali, the goddess of destruction. Feeding etiquette is minutely regulated. Cooked food must never pass up the chain of caste hierarchy; only raw food can be gifted to a Brahmin. Eating cannot be a shared or watched activity although no such taboo or shame attaches to elimination. Men and women eat separately at different times.

A Parsi family like ours in its comparative wealth and its Middle Eastern sense of hospitality views food as proof of God's bounty. To feed and be fed are synonymous in Parsi vocabulary with both pleasure and the Right Way. One can never visit a Parsi home without being overwhelmed with food. A normal Parsi wedding feast includes at a minimum fish steamed in banana leaf, eggs on tomatoes, chicken in gravy, vegetable stew, lamb roast, rice cooked with meat and fragrant spices, custard, *kulfi,* sweets and nuts, all of which are accompanied by pickles, yogurt and garnishes, served on tender banana leaves. During the great famine of 1877 it was a Parsi family that fed the city of Bombay for an entire eighteen months. As children we were taught to leave the last mouthful of food on the plate untouched. It was called "the mongrel's share" and was fed to stray animals. I always kept a rather large mouthful for those poor starving creatures.

I learned to cook under the exacting eye of my mother. She was a good cook but a lousy organizer. She pulled every pot and pan, dish and cover from every last shelf every time she prepared a meal. I was left to clear up the mess after she finished. And she criticized. Every move made by me or by the servant met with shrieks of disapproval. You had to peel carrots towards you, not away; and fry spices in a particular order. Potato skins had to come off in a perfect spiral from one end to the other. Fish had to be washed until it lost its fishy odors. Rice was rinsed until the water it stood in was pellucid. The magic number was seven: rice and lentils went through seven rinses, meats seven plus seven. And unless these formulae were followed, the meal would not turn out right. Once when I served her a meal I had cooked without her supervision she ran through a list of ingredients I might have left out and then the steps I might have omitted. When I denied any and all transgressions, she said flatly, "You cooked without love."

There are heating foods and cooling foods. You eat the first in the cold or wet months. In excess they cause boils and acne, much menstrual bleeding and sexual arousal. The cooling foods you eat in the hot months to cool both body and mind. Meat and nuts are heating, milk and rose petals cooling. And then there are categories of food reserved for convalescent children—rice, lentils and yogurt, all sprinkled with sugar. I dream about that combination of flavors after a meal of hamburger and fries.

TWO

She's pretty to walk with,
And witty to talk with,
And pleasant, too, to think on.
— Sir John Suckling

The older I grow, the more I like my mother and the more I am like her. I used to think my brother was her favorite. But I was wrong. When I was leaving home she said to me, "You are my eldest. I had to rely on you. I could not afford to let you be a child." She gave me complete responsibility for tasks at an age when other little girls just played. The younger children were handed over to me before I could manage their weight. I fed them and washed them. I talked to them to make sure that ghosts, who prey on wordless infants, would leave them alone in my voluble presence. I made up songs to sing to them. One that I composed for my brother was about a long journey the two of us would go on. The refrain was a litany of all the vehicles we would use, starting small with a bicycle and ending large with an airplane.

I started helping Mother in the kitchen as soon as I could carry a pot and learned to fold diapers in neat little triangles almost before I gave up wearing them. She was fastidious and unforgiving of error.

She would pinch my arm if I forgot a task. If I handed her the wrong pot or tool she tended to throw it at me. All the children were expert at dodging flying objects. I felt resentful but I never questioned or disobeyed her. A thoughtless teacher at school suggested that I might be a stepchild, which I hotly denied. That evening I stole the key to my father's steel almirah and rummaged through the papers until I found what I was looking for. I felt triumphant on seeing my mother's name clearly spelled out on my birth certificate.

One day when I was fifteen years old, my mother ordered me to sort the freshly laundered socks. For no apparent reason I said distinctly, "I won't." I could hear the blood singing in my ears, my mouth was utterly dry. I expected to be slapped for defiance. To my confusion and amazement, she did not say a word but merely picked up the socks and left the room. From that day on I could weather her wrath much better.

I was proud of my mother. She had been a high school teacher and gave it up only because of us. She taught while she was pregnant with me and harbored a sneaking suspicion that my academic brilliance had something to do with the headstart I had received *in utero.* My father always deferred to her superior knowledge in the areas of botany, zoology and children's infectious diseases.

Unlike other Indian women, Mother ran her household all by herself. Despised by her in-laws, isolated from her own kin, she struggled to be a model wife and mother. Hers was not a nature that compromised and she suffered intense frustration trying to reconcile her reality with her principles. Being the daughter of a priest, she was acutely conscious of cosmic pollution, but being the only adult female in the house, she could not observe the menstrual taboo to quarantine herself five days a month. The children had to be fed and the household chores done. So she drew arbitrary lines around objects and isolated them instead. The cupboard containing clothes to be worn to the fire temple could not be touched, nor the flower vases. She avoided handling pickles or new money. She purified us all with ritual baths when she emerged from her confinement.

Mother had unusual theories of child rearing, especially of character formation. No child was ever praised for fear of turning its head. On the contrary, to keep vanity at bay, she sought out a fatal flaw, real or imagined, in each of her children and constantly held it up for public scrutiny and ridicule. My lovely, fair sister who was named "moonface" for her beauty was told she lacked brains. My brother, a model student, was berated for his aggressiveness. I was reminded of my unrefined features and dark complexion. It took twenty-six years and an American male for me to find out that I have a dimple at the corner of my mouth when I smile. Failures were considered capital crimes, achievements went unremarked. The only word of praise I ever received from Mother was when I ranked first in the University at the baccalaureate examination. She said, "Congratulations, I am proud of you," and she hugged me, which embarrassed me terribly.

In spite of her circumstances, she was excellent at a lot of things. For one, she produced perfect babies. They did not look like wrinkled, red monkeys even in the hospital. They were beautiful with curved lashes and soft, ivory tinted skin. And her babies never smelled like soured milk. My father thought she was great in the kitchen and better in bed and shocked her by saying so aloud in front of her own father. But she was impossible to please most of the time. The day's shopping could never meet her exacting standards. If the green beans did not snap to attention or the spices make her sneeze as she sniffed them through the paper package they were considered stale. Her severest test was reserved for fish which had to enter her kitchen flapping its tail *in extremis.* To ensure this a pomfret's gill had to be pressed hard with a thumb before purchase. If what oozed out was white and viscous it was fresh, if red and watery it was to be given a wide berth. But this test had to be performed twice in a row because a fisherwoman was quite capable of daubing the white water from today's specimen onto yesterday's catch. Even coconuts had to be beheaded in her presence to ensure their edibility.

Mother operated on the principle that strangers were guilty until proven innocent, especially tradesmen whose sole goal in life was to cheat you. According to her, the tailor invariably kept back some of the material for himself and the grocer always short-weighted his goods; the goldsmith would switch the gem he was given to set, and the milk-seller add polluted water to his wares. Not even the purchase of a pet was exempt from such treachery by the seller. When Father decided to own a dog he purchased Leo, an Alsatian puppy with an impeccable pedigree. He was the offspring of the royal dam of the Maharaja of Alwar, but for Mother that was no guarantee. She took one look at the fluffy, duff-coloured animal, its tail wagging upright, its ears flopping downwards, and proclaimed it a mongrel. "Whoever saw an Alsatian with droopy ears?" she demanded, "They always carry their tails straight down, like wolves, and have an intelligent expression. You've been cheated again!" Father muttered something about not being present at the conception, and let it go. Three weeks later my two-year old sister burst into the room, excited beyond belief, shouting "Leo pointy ear!" And before we could figure that out, in trotted the animal with one ear irrefutably erect in a most Alsatian-like manner. Within a week the other ear followed suit and his expression definitely improved. Mother sheepishly acknowledged his genes but still cast doubt on his development.

The only person she did trust was the family jeweler. He was a Jain, and a strict adherent of that religion's creed of *ahimsa* as well as its rigorous food taboos. He had an old-fashioned office on the third floor of an ancient building. A dark and rickety staircase led to it from one of the narrowest and dirtiest lanes in Zaveri Bazaar. At the bottom of the stairwell we could observe fat rats, which were not only allowed to exist unmolested but fed regularly in line with the jeweler's ethic of charity to all living things. The office had mattresses on the floor, where both trader and customer sat cross-legged. He specialized in pearls. Whenever we went there with Mother, we would find Arab pearl-dealers from the Gulf, garbed in traditional robe and *keffiyeh.* After innumerable cups of coffee and a lot of Allahing, they would be ready for business. Clasping the jeweler's hand in their own they would throw a large checkered handkerchief over the joined hands. This would allow the two parties to quote and counter-quote in total privacy by counting off the figures on each other's fingers. The Indian traders, on the other hand, used secret words for numbers to hide their communication from any laymen present.

The jeweler had figured out Mother's *modus operandi.* He would show her a valuable gem. Mother would glance at it and ask, "How much?" When the price was out in the open she would scrutinize it more closely and list its faults: "Look! there's a web in it, and I can see a carbon spot. Doesn't the color fade out in the upper corner?" she would mumble *sotto voce,* holding the jeweler's loop like a pirate's patch over her eye. Immediately he would agree with all her criticisms, adding, "Perhaps this one's not for you." Then Mother would start feeling her way to a compromise. Her head cocked on one side, she would offer to take the gem off his hands at one third the quoted price. Smilingly he would decline. But he could read the avarice in her eyes and knew he had a sale, no matter the number of feints Mother would throw, or the hours more it would take to clinch the deal.

I remember clearly the way we built her pearl necklace one pearl at a time. For six days in a row Mother and I went to the jeweler's in the morning. His sister heaped a measureful of pearls on a low stool in front of us. Mother methodically worked her way through the pile. With the same gesture she used to cull a trayful of rice before cooking it, she flicked apart a few pearls at a time from the heap. Out of these she picked the one that was perfectly round, just the right tone of blush, the luminosity of its water creating an uninterrupted aura sheathing its roundness. The remainder were pushed aside with a sweeping motion of the side of the hand. She went through many cullings without picking a single one. As morning turned to afternoon and afternoon to evening, she absent-mindedly sipped the cups of tea and nibbled at the snacks offered to us, her mind's eye never wandering from the finished string. On the seventh day we could rest in the knowledge of a perfect task completed perfectly. Because of the memory of that string of pearls I am content with mere trinkets for myself.

Despite her mistrust of people's motives Mother was genuinely curious about human nature. She made friends easily and could sympathize with the plight of total strangers. She once bought a mousetrap from a peddler who had knocked on the door. The man reappeared the next day, trying to sell another one to her. "We have only one mouse!" said Mother, as she sent the man on his way. The day after he was back, and the next as well. Finally, Mother lost her temper and threatened to call the police. "But I have to see you first thing in the morning," explained the mousetrap-seller. "You are a very lucky customer for me. The day you bought a trap from me, I sold a dozen. Please let me glimpse your auspicious face regularly and I will supply you with free mousetraps forever." This mollified Mother, and she obliged the man for the next few days by stepping out on the veranda whenever she heard the clappity-clap clacking of the mousetrap-seller in the street.

Mother's worst side was on display in her altercations with the servants, when we had any. In a Parsi household servants fall into two categories. There is the young male kitchen-help and errand boy who is referred to generically as "Rama," and a female who washes the dishes and does the daily laundry, known as "Ganga". In mythology, Siva, married to Parvati, took Ganga as his mistress. She was quiet and beautiful but of low caste. In villages Brahmins still take their concubines from the lowest castes. "I am Parvati, not Ganga," said one of our servants indignantly. Mother was not at all convinced. No pretty Ganga was ever employed. They were to be seen at work, preferably without pause, but they were not to be heard from. Those that called our sitting-room an assembly hall or its ceiling church rafters, or those who said our home was a madhouse, were instantly dismissed. Mother's steady stream of Gangas came in all shades of color, caste and political opinions. There was the fat one whose husband had branded her on her cheek for impudence a month after her marriage at twelve. Gopi had just arrived from a village and had not yet heard of Mother's reputation as an employer. There was another with an exaggerated fear of dogs. She sidled past the neighbor's Alsatian, her hands folded prayerfully in front of her face, chanting "Caesar, Caesar, do not bite me!" Jethibai was the old hereditary bathroom-cleaner. She entered and left the house strictly through the doors, and in one case a window, of the various bathrooms, since she was an untouchable. But Mother let her sit on the bedroom floor and drink tea out of a cracked cup set aside specially for her as she gossiped about her other clients. And we can never forget Mother-in-law, who was six foot tall with teeth protruding like tusks. She came to work with her daughter whom she proceeded to feed secretly with food from the kitchen. When accused of theft by Father she drew herself up and replied, "That is not thieving! I took, but only according to my needs." "Now we have a bloody Marxist one!" spluttered Father. Most of Mother's servants barely lasted a week, and some decamped at the end of the first day, not waiting even to collect their wage.

On the rare occasions when Mother was not busy cleaning or criticizing she could be most charming and gracious. She would gather us around her and recite poetry to us—Sir Walter Scott, Keats, Wordsworth. In her high-pitched voice with its Indian cadence, she made it sound like an incantation. "Gather ye rosebuds while ye may", she would enunciate, pronouncing the buds as if it were "birds", and would smile tolerantly when we asked how a rose-bird's song sounded. At other times, as we clustered around her on the sofa, she slowly turned the leaves of old German calendars with reproductions of classics by Leonardo da Vinci, Dürer and Rembrandt. She would pause to draw our attention to the realism of a bee clinging to a flower in a still life or the light suffusing a Dutch landscape. She never threw away any of these old calendars and stored an entire collection under her mattress to prevent the edges from curling. Her favorite was Vermeer's "Girl at a Window." She shared with us her enthusiasms and inculcated in us a critical eye for form, line and grace. I can still hear her clear voice on the terrace calling, "Come children, hurry! You will miss the sunset."

One of Mother's favorite pastimes was to construct elaborate designs out of her collection of gems. At the end of her morning in the kitchen, her frayed housecoat stained with turmeric, she unlocked the secret compartment of the trompe l'oeil almirah. This was quite a feat because it involved sprawling on the floor and reaching underneath for an upside-down keyhole. Carefully she would remove her unset diamonds, rubies and emeralds meticulously folded in yellow or blue glazed paper squares lined with tissue. With a secret smile she would bend lovingly over her stones, content to spend an entire afternoon arranging them into necklaces or earrings. Sometimes they had rubies for centers, sometimes emeralds. They always looked faintly floral or had arabesques like those on the ceilings of the Jain temples at Mount Abu. When she had an arrangement she particularly liked, she would call us in to give our verdict.

My mother was the eldest of six daughters of a small-town priest of modest means. We knew our grandmother only through a sepia tint. She was a grave and aristocratic-looking woman. Mother avoided talking about her. The calumny of bearing six females in a row had driven Grandmother to frequent suicide attempts. Grandfather had tried to distract her by taking her on holidays, but he had to earn a living. Her own family would not assume responsibility for her since an Indian daughter, once married, belongs to her in-laws. In desperation her husband confined her to an institution where she was chained and beaten to drive out her possessing demons.

Grandfather did not visit us frequently, for he hated to take sides in my parents' squabbles. He was full of clever sayings. Dressed in starched white muslin ceremonial garb, he boasted about his vigorous health. At the end of his visit he tipped each servant more than what he usually got paid for performing a marriage. I don't think he really liked children. In another social station he would have been a club man. Nevertheless, he told us stories and made us memorize rhyming riddles. At seventy-six he went on a hiking trip to the Himalayas and on his return promptly recorded the experience in a published travelog.

I am sure Mother felt herself an unloved child at home. At the age of four she was sent off to her maternal grandparents' estate near the sea. Her grandfather owned twenty-eight villages and no one had measured his holdings, not even the revenue officers. Part of the estate included a virgin forest where her blue-eyed Grandpa went boar or tiger shooting. The only certain thing was that it took a man three days to ride across the family's holdings. Here with dozens of her cousins, she grew up an indulged grandchild who everyone wished had been a son. She had her own goat and drank all the milk it gave straight from the fat-bellied brass pot in which it was brought to the house. She had her own pear tree where she retreated with a bowl of fruit and a book. Once when her uncle's eldest son threatened to invade her tree, she kicked him off a branch. He had to wear his arm in a sling for a long time. For sport Mother killed sparrows with the brass buckle of a long leather belt. As the birds circled around the high-ceilinged storeroom seeking relief from the scorching noonday sun, she waited belt in hand for them. She became such an expert that it only took one quick twirl to bring them down. Most of the time she merely broke their legs. When at the age of thirty-five she became crippled with arthritis, she accepted it as divine justice.

Mother's boldness endeared her to her grandfather, a short, peppery man who was something of a domestic tyrant. Mother insisted that his authority was so absolute that before going on to the stables, even the carriage horses paused and bowed to him as he sat on the veranda. Mother, however, was permitted to take liberties with his whiskers. When he went on a successful tiger shoot, she was allowed to pluck out the eyes of the prize. And once, in the company of his male friends, he got her drunk on toddy. When asked what she wanted to do when she was grown up, Mother recklessly declared she would become a lawyer. Her grandmother worried about her independent nature. No mother-in-law would stand for so much spirit, she would warn. One day, hoping to get her interested in womanly things, Grandmother let her dress up in her hand-embroidered Chinese silk *sari* and her pair of dangling emerald earrings. Forgetting she had the finery on, Mother chased a cousin down to the beach. One of the earrings fell off. Her grandmother sifted the sand with a rice sieve for three days, but the earring was never found.

The idyll could not last forever and Mother was sent back to her parent's home to help look after her younger sisters as her own mother withdrew further from reality. She was not allowed to finish school but she would do it anyway in the future, although it would cost her a marriage and a child.

Mother was a Theosophist. This pseudo-religious movement, the brainchild of Madame Blavatsky, appealed to a lot of intellectual Indians simply because it was so eclectic a system. It certainly fascinated Parsis because it was based on a free and unacknowledged borrowing of the dualistic principles of Zoroastrianism, to which were added the familiar Hindu ideas of *karma* and the transmigration of the soul. When I read a biography of Blavatsky, I was shocked to see how ruthlessly this charlatan had manipulated a generation of high-minded Indians.

Mother was too discriminating to adopt anything wholesale. What drew her to Theosophy was an idealistic search for the existence of a "higher self." She wanted to believe that there were evolved spirits just as there were evolved species, and that an individual could participate actively in his own spiritual self-evolution. By the time we arrived on the scene, Mother was no longer directly involved in the movement, thanks to Father's loud and vociferous ridiculing of the whole enterprise. But she occasionally lapsed into talk of "her master" who existed not in the flesh but as a spirit guide. When we asked how it was possible to exist only in spirit she turned to some Victorian proof in support of her position. There were, she insisted, photographs of spirit beings. For example, an English photographer had accidentally caught on film an angel that could not resist jumping over a skipping rope after a line of children. The camera being able to see everything, had captured that which was invisible to our inferior perceptions. We remained skeptical: what was the angel wearing? we asked her, and were its wings folded or spread out when it jumped over the rope? And why did it not just fly over the thing? She clucked in exasperation and said we were not evolved enough to understand. I gave her the benefit of the doubt and conceded that angels just might exist. I imagined an angel would look something like the curly headed tot in Pears soap advertisements sporting a pair of gauze wings like those used in school plays, minus the soap bubbles, of course.

Father fed us more down-to-earth information. On the long daily commute to and from school we got a steady stream of information. We learned about the world. Question: Where does petrol come from? Answer: Crushed trees and dinosaurs. We heard Parsi myths. "There was a time when the community desperately needed a new fire temple but did not have the funds for it. A Zoroastrian priest, pure of body and spirit, locked himself in a room with copper ingots. At the end of the week, a worried community broke down the door to find that the priest had totally disappeared, but the room was filled with light from the heap of gold." When Father was in a bad temper we had to recite our multiplication tables up to 20 times 20. When he was jovial we asked him questions: What is the rainbow made of? Why is the number 7 magical and 13 unlucky? How long is an elephant pregnant? He always answered every question.

Father bought every educational toy on the market. We had puzzles that taxed our ingenuity and chemistry sets that made interesting fizzing noises when we combined the contents. For my sister, he got Russian poetry books in translation. These flooded the sidewalk book market when India signed a friendship treaty with Russia in the 1950's. We enjoyed the foreign children's names, like Vova and Kira and Alexandrova. As I remember, the poems were rather didactic and very much in the vein of *Strumwelpeter.* Because I liked to write, he bought me expensive stationery and allowed me to choose fountain pens from his extensive personal collection. He was the only parent in the entire school who came to watch us perform in school plays or recite our own poems in front of our classmates. He was always willing to help us memorize our roles as, script in hand, he corrected our pronunciations and instructed us on the finer points of declamation.

Some information, however, was considered unnecessary for children. We were deliberately kept ignorant of death and sex on the grounds that it would be like giving eyes to the blind, where blindness served to protect and prevent. When my little sister accidentally bathed herself in kerosene and drank some for good measure from the supply for the primus stove, I wondered how things would change for her if she died. She looked cherubic and very flushed as she lay in the cot after the doctor's visit. I thought heaven would have thousands of such beautiful, glowing little girls. Mother strongly disapproved of children at funerals. She would refer to the case of a cousin who was made to view her father's corpse when she was only six and, as a result, had her intelligence permanently affected. She did seem to us rather dull-witted and fearful.

As for sex, it did not exist.

THREE

Could the memory but hold!
— All the sunsets, flushed with gold
—James Stephens

When I think of home, I think of the bungalow at Pali Hill. It was in the suburbs overlooking the ocean. Pali Hill was an enclave of two minorities, the Christians and the Parsis. The former lived at the foot of the hill in small houses. We grew up viewing them as inferiors, first because most of them are descended from converts of the lowest castes and still carry the stigma of their Hindu past, and secondly because the rest of them are Anglo-Indians and are perceived as half-breeds who, while being of two worlds, belong to neither. We found their aping of English customs such as kissing in public amusing or embarrassing.

The large estates at the top of the hill were owned by Parsis with a few still in European possession. From this height one gets an unimpeded view of the coast line and the ocean a mile away. At one end of this bay is the fishing village of Danda. In the summer months the entire village and much of the sea shore is covered with bamboo scaffolds on which Bombay ducks are hung to dry in the sun, their fishy scent pervading the entire island. Bombay duck is a soft white fish with edible bones that melts in the mouth. Deep fried, it is a delicacy much relished in Parsi households. Father bought these only on Sundays and it signalled a truce between my parents. He ate them with fried eggs and raw onion and each child got a tidbit from his plate.

There was only one narrow road over the hill and the local buses terminated at the bottom. The climb was steep and at the first turn the temperature fell sharply as one headed into the sea breeze. The road then passed the little church whose bells marked the passing of each hour. On that corner stood the Green Bungalow, the only house on Pali Hill owned by Muslims. It had high walls surrounding it and the main gate was guarded by a Pathan in a *pugree* who always salaamed to Papa. We sometimes glimpsed women in *burqas* strolling deep in a verdant garden. Slightly further on was the little white Anglican church whose bells rang out the Angelus. The sound of church bells makes me feel at home immediately anywhere in the world.

The bungalow we grew up in was right at the top of the hill. Built by an Englishman at the turn of the century, it was bought by a Parsi aesthete. It snuggled on one side of the hill and had a massive fortress of a foundation with sloping sides, much like villas clinging to the cliffs along the road from Amalfi to Sorrento. The bungalow came with several acres including a formal garden, orchard and tropical forest. It had three Baccarat chandeliers in the main salon which was so large that we learned to bicycle around its periphery. A long balcony, like a ship's deck, faced the sea with forty-five double windows giving a panoramic view. My brother and I started at opposite ends of the balcony each morning opening the windows and raced to meet at the center. In the evenings we raced to close them before the mosquitoes swarmed in for their nightly feast of our blood. A large open terrace extended from the balcony. Its floor was white terrazzo bordered in blue, and long French doors with translucent etched glass opened onto it. Day after day, year after year, we watched the sunsets from that terrace, no two ever alike. In the summer the sky turned different shades of red, from cerise and vermilion to coral and salmon, and the sun slipped like a golden guinea into the water. During the monsoons its hues were mauve and lilac. Dark waves leapt up to grab at darker clouds racing to meet the land. And the sun, ragged-edged, faded from sight high above the horizon. One rainy evening we saw a perfect circle rainbow holding a pale watery sun in its embrace. At night, the light from a full moon glanced off each tessera, turning the terrace into a shimmering lake. The ocean breeze at high tide was so strong that ninety windows swayed on their hinges in unison and the terrace doors had to be immobilized with great chunks of marble. The floors throughout the house were designed to feel cool to hot feet, from the classic black and white marble in the study to the red hexagonal terracotta, reminiscent of a Sevillian courtyard, in the rest of the house.

The bungalow was cavernously large. In order to aid the flow of air, the main floor had twenty-four-foot high ceilings with huge exposed crossbeams supporting the tiled roof. The space was divided into three wings, one of which became the children's dormitory. The kitchen and servants' quarters were detached from the main house but connected to it by a covered passageway. There was a stable converted to a garage, gardener's sheds and store rooms. It would normally take six or eight servants to run that place. Mother frequently had none. A wickedly steep slope with two hairpin bends led from the main iron gates to the covered portico. Once, when returning from school, Father put the car in neutral and walked out to open the gates. The car, with four children and the day's shopping in it, started rolling gently forward. Father made a heroic effort to stop the car by stepping in front of it but of course it kept rolling. At the first turn it slipped off the drive and into the branches of a big, old mango tree where it halted. We climbed down from the tree unhurt. Father decided he had to be on God's right side, for not only were his children unharmed, but not a single egg of the dozen carried in the back seat was broken. Until a crane could arrive on the scene, a steady stream of servants from the neighboring houses came to see the car that had climbed a tree.

When we first arrived at the bungalow it was furnished with art from around the world. There were Florentine paintings, carved oriental teak inlaid with ivory, Chinese jade and Venetian glass. Even the flower pots in the fernery were hand-painted Japanese porcelain. One large painting particularly caught my mother's fancy. It showed a young semi-draped woman in red velvet lying on a chaise longue with her back to the viewer while an infant played with a Negress on the floor. The painting had the sentiments of an Ingres. Mother offered to buy it; the owner preferred to sell the entire contents as one lot to a junk dealer who trundled it all away, piled pell-mell in his rusty wheelbarrow with its wobbly iron wheels. Nevertheless, Mother rescued a very good Impressionist landscape framed in carved walnut and a small ivory-inlaid tea table from the top of the heap.

The owner had been a wealthy solicitor who had never married. When he died his housekeeper, a young widow with a daughter, inherited the property. She was reputed to have been a beauty in her youth and the daughter might have been the solicitor's, or so the old gardener said. She did have milk white skin and a lot of verve in her nineties. She got into screaming matches with her servants. Once she requested the maid to help her out of her seat and prop her up so she could kick a recalcitrant sweeper woman.

Her daughter, who was in her late sixties, dyed her hair a bright red, had studied art on the Left Bank, and always wore a snuff-brown chiffon *sari* whose loose end she wrapped around her throat à la Isadora Duncan. She would walk around the house sighing and trying to revive the ghosts of her youth: the tea parties, the card games on the terrace, the dinners under the chandeliers. It seemed as if the two women's lives had abruptly ended when the solicitor died. They left the house unused for years before my father was able to talk them into renting it to him. The only time they came to the house was in the fruit season to collect the mangoes and jackfruit.

The bungalow was so remote that we had almost no visitors. Mother often complained that she was imprisoned in that vast place. The only diversion was afforded by the itinerant vendors and tradesmen on their annual rounds. Of the former I remember the macaroni-seller. He came with a huge iron trunk which was neatly divided into compartments inside. Each square held pasta squiggles of a different size or color. He also carried some *papad* and rice-flour curls for his less westernized customers. Mother prolonged her haggling with him, and when neither was looking we would run our fingers through the goods to hear the click of fat pasta shells striking each other. The Muslim egg seller came thrice a week, but he was severe, and would not deign to negotiate or indulge in idle chatter.

Once a year the roofers would appear to tar the seams in the tiled roof. They brought antiquated mobile furnaces to heat the tar, and the not unpleasant smell would last for days. The tropical sun prevented the tar from hardening and made it flow in little rivulets which ended in shiny black blobs. We would sneak onto the roof to break these off and use them as jacks for our games. If we weren't careful the tar would stick to our bare feet, and no amount of scrubbing would remove the evidence or prevent the punishment which followed.

At infrequent intervals the mattress-maker would show up. All the mattresses in the home would be disembowelled and the cotton stuffing beaten to make it fluff up again. He used the most peculiar gadget to do this: it consisted of a solid wood piece like a rounded hourglass and a length of bamboo with grooves cut in it over which were stretched sheep-gut strings. A handful of cotton would be twanged against the strings with this device till the wad broke up into clouds of wafting fluff, which sent us into fits of sneezing. When the furniture polisher appeared he stripped down the old finish to the naked wood before reapplying a glorious smelling chocolate-colored ooze with his bare fingers to the teak and mahogany. There were also the smiths who came to tin the heavy copper cooking vessels whose linings wore out regularly from repeated scrubbing with coconut husks. Mother would deputize a child to stand over them, since they had a habit of absconding with the valuable pots. For a few days afterwards the kitchen rack gleamed with a silvery sheen even in the dark.

Father rented the house without telling anyone about it. One day we had gone to school as usual. Mother was given the car, the chauffeur, a stack of money and sent off to the city to shop. Father ordered two trucks and twenty men from the Mills and everything was carried from the old house to the new in six hours. There was no packing before nor unpacking after. Besides, he had bought a lot of new furniture which was delivered directly to the bungalow. After school, we were taken over unfamiliar roads and up a hill to the house. Mother was similarly delivered by the chauffeur to the new address. I think she was delighted with the view but it rankled her that she had not been consulted and her approval not obtained before the move. For twenty years she groused about Father's arbitrariness, the remoteness of the bungalow's location and the ugliness of the new, heavy, leather furniture.

Because of this experience, I grew up believing that women had nothing to do with the procurement of living space. When I had to go looking for a home of my own I felt terribly resentful. "This is not a woman's job," I kept repeating to myself. But I did not trust a man to do it for me. I wanted a house that felt like Pali Hill, spacious and full of light, although I knew I could not afford the view. Since then I have found my house and I have worked steadily to transmute it to echoes from my childhood.

FOUR

Whatever he says is law,
whatever he gives is alms

— Persian proverb

The pictures of my father that I carry in my mind are so vivid and powerful that they reduce me instantly to a child whenever I think of him. Time and distance have failed to dim even the earliest of these images.

There I am, clinging to his stomach chimp-fashion as he sits on the small wood swing hung on the door-frame of our first home. The sun beats down on the open veranda. Its iron railing casts a shadow-grid on the stone floor, making it undulate. As he swings back and forth, I feel overpowered with sensation: giddiness from the motion, heat from his body and its sweetish-sour smell, the scratchiness of his muslin shirt on which I rest my cheek and the flashes of brilliant yellow behind tightly shut eyelids as we move from sunlight into shade and back again. I dislike the sound of my mother's voice which cuts short this first remembered moment with my father.

There are other pictures of the two of us etched just as clearly. I feel my head being stroked in my sleep. Through half-open eyes I see the window is dark. Father who never dresses in anything but white drill pants and pin-striped shirts is standing over me wearing a suit, tie and solar *topee.* I realize it is the day of his monthly plane trip to the textile mills in Ahmedabad. I know Mother will be difficult all day until his return late at night. He will bring home the rubbery red and green, cashew-studded sweet that is made only in that sooty, hot city. At the door he turns and winks at me and I am certain all of a sudden that no man can ever be as handsome as my father.

There I am with him in the kitchen sharing the quiet companionability of a Sunday afternoon spent polishing the brass cooking stoves while the rest of the house drowses. And then of course, I see him in his annual role playing octopus, ten fingers holding open a text book at ten different places for my last-second review before I walk into the examination hall. The nervousness of his expression belies the bravado of his pep talk.

But more immediate than any of these images is the sound of my father. His full-throated whistling can fill up space like an entire orchestra. His singing voice is equally lush. A melody of Schubert or Strauss as it comes from him sums up for me all that is right with this world. Once an Indian film producer, hearing him singing, tried to offer him a contract via the servant working in the garden. That good man had enough presence of mind to retort, "My Master sings wonderfully but can swear even better. Besides, he is rich enough to buy several producers like you." On rare occasions, he would sing a classical Indian raga and then, Mother proudly attested, he sounded like Saigal, the legendary singer of Urdu love songs.

My father's personality bears the mark of being a widow's son. He was born into a wealthy family. His physician father died when Father was only a couple of months old. In spite of being just twenty-one, beautiful and wealthy, his mother refused remarriage and willingly observed ritual mourning until she died in her eighties. I saw her twice in my life, once to invite her to my initiation and the second time when I left the country. My brother and I dubbed her "Puck" because she was tiny and exotic and wore slippers that resembled those we had seen in illustrations of Shakespeare by the Pre-

Raphaelites. Father had spoken only ill of her and so I was not disposed to any friendly overtures except those required by politeness towards strangers.

She was the adopted daughter of a diamond merchant. Her natural father had been a millwright with a family of 21 children. Although he earned only 45 rupees a month, he was too proud to allow any woman of his family to go to the river to fetch water, and so had a tank built behind his house to store rainwater. The wealthy of the town of Broach saw this as snobbery above his station. Grandmother was four when her father's brother, the jeweler, came for a visit. He was married but childless. Right away uncle and niece became inseparable, and at the end she went to see him off at the railway station. When he took his seat she climbed onto his lap and refused to get off. No one and nothing could persuade her to let go of her uncle. Finally, as the whistle blew, he offered to take her with him to Bombay for a few days, promising to send her back with a servant the moment she showed signs of homesickness. She stayed for the rest of her life. When she was widowed it was perfectly natural for her to go back to her childhood home, contrary to the usual practice. Her mother felt ambiguous about harboring such an inauspicious person under her roof, but her father welcomed her back without hesitation. Had she shown the slightest inclination to remarry he would have willingly provided a second dowry from his ample fortune.

It was pure accident that had led the old man to his lucrative trade. He had started as a common navvy on the Gujarat railway. The work paid well but was arduous beyond belief. The heat was so intense that he avoided a sunstroke only by wrapping his head in a sopping wet bedsheet that would turn bone-dry by lunchtime. At the end of the contract, with spare change in his pocket, he splurged on a ruby ring for himself. Then for a while he became an apprentice hat-maker constructing the elaborate Parsi chintz *khoka*. It involved securing each layer of stiff shiny material to the frame with metal tacks. One day as he was working a customer stopped to watch him. His eye caught the gleam of the ruby ring on the craftsman's hand and he offered to buy it on the spot. "My personal belongings are not for sale," said Great-Grandfather curtly as he continued with the job. But as he started to hammer in the next tack his hand slipped and the hammer split the ruby in half. Trying to turn this irony of fate into some kind of good portent he went to the Zaveri Bazaar, the jewelers' market, to find a replacement. Now, it is next to impossible to find an exact replica of a colored gem. But during his long search Great-Grandfather became fascinated with all gems and started picking up the knowledge and lore of this business. From that point on it seemed he had found his niche, and he became a prosperous and respected trader in that bazaar. A little later he formed a syndicate with two other partners, one in Amsterdam and the other an Englishman in Calcutta. The latter took to drink and gambling and eventually died leaving business debts for which the others were liable. In spite of this Great-Grandfather sought out the man's widow and supported her for the rest of her life. He established such a name for himself that wealthy families in the community came to him to put together their girls' dowries. But none of his clients was worthy of the choicest gems, which he saved for his own beautiful but unlucky daughter. Father would sometimes be moved to describe to us these exquisite pieces of jewelry that belonged to his mother. We never saw them and never will since on her death Grandmother left our inheritance to the *Ashram* of the fakir Mehr Baba. Father says he is going to leave all his wealth to charity as well.

Of my paternal grandfather, I have very little knowledge. I have seen his photograph, a European-looking gentleman in dress and mien except for his eyes which are dark and identical in expression to those of his son. Grandfather was brilliant. He passed his medical exams at the first try, which turned out to be a professional drawback because the general public at that time believed that the more often a young man failed at his exams the longer the period he would spend as an intern, and hence the more mature and experienced a doctor he would emerge at the end. The only openings available to someone like my grandfather were those considered undesirable by the six- and seven-times failed. He ended up as a ship's doctor.

All on board took him for a Sahib till at sunset he stood on deck and pulled out his shirt-tails in order to perform his evening prayers. He was known for his hair-trigger temper. When a Hindu classmate in the medical college kept on teasing him about it in spite of repeated warnings, he decided to teach the fellow a lesson. The final year students were allowed to use the morgue without supervision. So one day Grandfather with two other Parsi classmates invited the Hindu to finish up their assignments in the morgue. Old Abdullah who kept the keys was told that they had a lot of catching up to do and would therefore sign themselves out very late. They assured him that the keys would be left in the customary place, and there was no need for him to wait.

Next morning Abdullah came as usual to set things up. As he walked through the door of the morgue he saw to his horror a cadaver slide off a dissecting table and begin to hop towards him. He turned and fled gibbering all the way to the Principal's office. Apparently Grandfather with the help of his friends had lashed the Hindu to a stiff and left him in that cold gruesome place all night, from where the unfortunate fellow was trying to hop his way out. So shocking had the experience been that it actually unhinged his mind. The Principal rusticated the culprits on the spot and barred them from appearing for the final exams. This meant a waste of seven years of hard work and an end to their hopes of practicing medicine. The ringleader's father happened to be the Principal of the Elphinstone High School, the first and most prestigious native educational institution in Bombay. He was acquainted in his official capacity with the Governor. So he called on His Excellency and without a word laid his hat at the Governor's feet. Startled and impressed by this unheard-of gesture of supplication from so erudite a man, the Governor granted a pardon with a proviso: the three could appear for the coming exams but if they failed there would be no second chance. Then Great-Grandfather returned home and thrashed the boys within an inch of their lives. Needless to add, they all managed to pass on the first attempt, a feat considered quite extraordinary at that time.

The doctor, my father's father, was a connoisseur known for his rich tastes. He owned a collection of walking sticks including one with a solid gold knob with which he is said to have knocked a pickpocket unconscious in the gutter. One morning in surgery he was infected with meningitis; fifteen hours later he was dead. He left behind him a legacy of unhappiness that has not yet run out.

The widow renounced the world and withdrew into her children. Her son especially became the focus of her overwhelming grief. She guarded him with a ferocious discipline. He was not allowed any physical activity because "children who swim drown, and those who bicycle fall off and die of blood poisoning." His day was carefully monitored, his toys were locked up and he was allowed only an hour a week to play with them. He told us how he would have to beg for the key to his favorite toy, a nineteenth century masterpiece of the clockwork-maker's art. It consisted of a cage with trees and birds in it. When activated, the little forest came alive with the whirring of wings and the warbling of the gilded birds. There is one just like it in the Smithsonian. When the boy finally rebelled against the tyranny of her love and fled from home, the mother kept every toy, together with his nursery books, wrapped in shrouds, inside tall dark cupboards.

Although Grandmother had returned to her parents' home, she did not get along with her own mother. That lady's capacity for quarrels and her distrust of her own species were legendary. She possessed a herbal remedy that dissolved cataracts. She prepared it with much labor once a year. But she locked herself into a room for the duration of the work and even her own husband, who was deputed to fetch the ingredients, was unsure whether the recipe in fact called for everything she ordered. She refused to part with her secret and a valuable folk remedy died with her. Her distrust extended to her own daughter. She vilified the poor girl for being a widow and found her very presence in the home a calamity. Father described to us how the household resounded with their name-calling.

His only ally in this female bastion was his grandfather, an indulgent and mild mannered man who prescribed retreat in the face of womanly assault or tears. Every morning the old man had escorted the child to school, but on the walk there the boy cried and pleaded not to be left at that awful place where the schoolmistress placed him on her knee and kissed him in front of the rest of the children. So back they walked home again dreading what awaited them. The older woman would round on her husband and berate him for weakness of will. The mother would work at disengaging the child clinging to the window bars by rapping the knuckles of each hand in turn with a cane. He would then be sent right back, this time with a servant who had strict orders to use physical force if necessary to leave him in the classroom. Once he graduated to the boys' school with its Victorian schoolmasters, he had no further problems. In fact, next to his own grandfather, Father most revered his high school principal.

Cassim, the servant, was also partial to Father. He served the family for forty years. It is probable that he was an illegitimate child of a Parsi father and a low-caste Hindu mother from one of the small *mofussil* towns. Father described him as fat, jovial, and black as the ace of spades. Every month on payday out of his meager salary of fifteen rupees he took Father and his sister to the zoo. On top of footing the admission charge, he paid for the elephant and camel rides and bought both children ice-cream cones to end the afternoon. Of the two children, Father was Cassim's favorite. Whenever he went to the neighborhood saloon for a drink, he brought father back a generous handful of roasted grams, which were served free with the beer. Since both kids vied for the bone marrow from the evening's roast, Cassim devised a trick for Father's benefit: he would feed the marrow to the boy in the afternoon and restuff the empty bone with mashed white pumpkin flavored with meat extract. At dinnertime he would make a great show of extracting it and serving it to the girl. It took her years to catch on. Cassim earned instant extra cash equal to his monthly salary if he found and returned any gem dropped accidentally by Great-Grandfather in his home office. Father would let Cassim claim credit for any he himself retrieved from the cracks in the floors.

When talking about his childhood Father never mentioned any other children or playmates. It seems he was brought up in a circle of elite Parsi adults, not a few of whom were pioneers and leaders in their fields. His musical talent was fostered by no less than the courtly Lady Palamkote who single-handedly introduced the native gentry to Western classical music. She was a gifted pianist and of course taught several generations of younger musicians. It was her solo performance that capped the Bombay musical season. The recital was always attended by the Honorable Governor of Bombay Presidency, for whom a special red wool carpet was rolled all the way out to the curb. Her younger sister acted as stage assistant, but she could not read music. So Lady Palamkote would signal to her to turn the page by officiously clearing her throat. The final piece or encore was usually Scriabin's nocturne for the left hand, which she played holding her right hand dramatically behind her back. She donated her entire earnings to set up a scholarship for Indian students at the Trinity College of Music in London.

Then there were the two fabulously rich sisters who were close friends of his mother. They were famous for their skill at setting broken bones, an art which is still practiced in India by a traditional caste rather than by medical doctors. They charged no fees and consequently had so many clients that they worked well past midnight daily. The older of the two kept the mobs in order with a steady stream of the most unladylike oaths. When they heard that our grandmother, their friend, refused to attend our initiation, the sisters came in full regalia as representatives from Father's side of the family. I remember being dazzled by the diamond necklaces that covered their bosoms as they sat, honored guests, in the first row. I think

Father was touched and grateful for their display of loyalty and tried to spend as much time as he could with them that busy evening.

Father's relationship with his sister was and has remained one of petty rivalry. She confided in us once that as a child he would throw tantrums if their mother so much as turned her face towards the daughter as she sat between her children to sew or read. Grandmother claimed that her son was brilliant but uncontrollable, her daughter dull but faithful. Each child played out its expected destiny to perfection. My aunt was quiet and did not do too well at school. I think she realized and accepted quite early in life that, given her brother's temperament, it would have to be her lot to look after their mother in her old age. She therefore did not encourage suitors in her youth. Father mocked her when he found her reading Victorian tracts with titles like "On the Virtue of Duty" and "Solace to the Sick at Heart." He has never understood or appreciated her sacrifice which left him free to pursue his own desires away from the expectations and demands of his mother.

My aunt apprenticed with a homeopath and eventually practiced as one herself. It was touching to see how she had appropriated her physician father's brass nameplate by squeezing her own initial in front of his name. Now that Grandmother is dead, my aunt lives alone, following every rule and precept the old woman had ever lain down and measuring the days in terms of prayers and rituals to be performed for her departed mother's soul.

Father prides himself on his rock-like firmness of purpose. He would often boast how once he made up his mind he could not be shaken from his course, and offered as proof his marriage to Mother. He first saw her as he stood with friends and family to welcome the new bride of a neighbor. On catching a glimpse of her he turned to his grandfather and said, "There is the girl I am going to marry." The old man laughed at this silly notion, pointing out that she was in fact the new bride. "You wait and see," said Father, and although it took him ten years and the renunciation of a fortune, he did in fact marry her.

Mother had a slightly different version. "This impertinent young fellow kept knocking at my door asking to borrow needle, thread or some such for his sister or mother," she recalled. When she quickly became disillusioned with the husband her family had chosen for her, she started to view the youth differently. They went through a seven year courtship which Mother claimed was mostly against her wishes. Before they could marry, she had to dissolve her first marriage, which included giving up her daughter, then finish her college education, and find a way to support herself. He had somehow to get a degree, a task made almost impossible for this once prize student because of his passionate involvement.

Appalled at the thought of her only son marrying a divorcée, his mother drove him out of her home and her life. She disinherited him and had him fired from his job on the grounds of disobedience towards her. The couple had to meet clandestinely on deserted beaches and desolate hillocks which they fondly pointed out to us. The courtship was as rocky as their trysting places. "She was always late," he complained; "He stepped on my wristwatch in rage," she remembered, adding that that should have warned her never to marry him. He wrote her sonnets and poems that he could still quote to us from memory twenty years later, especially the one that sounded like Wordsworth's "Daffodils." She penned him parables glorifying love and sacrifice. I watched her burn both collections in the garden over several hours on the day he filed for a divorce from her.

They were married out of town, she in the cheapest cotton *sari*, he in shirt sleeves. Grandmother was embittered and unforgiving when she learned of the event from a list of marriages published in the newspapers. Mother never wore her thin wedding ring, Father never took his off. They started housekeeping in a rented room near the airport. This area was just being reclaimed from swamp and was infested with insects. After dinner, they pulled down the mosquito curtain on the bed, sprayed the enclosed space with Flit, and went for a walk. When they returned, the white bed sheet would have turned black from the dead mosquitoes littering it. She started working at a school, he at a textile factory. His pride was stung at the humiliation of his first job there. He had to wash out the dye-stuff drums. The old illiterate teaching him the ropes assured the apprentice dyeing-master that one day soon he would be giving orders to hundreds of underlings like himself—and the old man was right. Between them, the couple made barely enough to get through to the end of the month. Father described the ritual they devised to survive the fourth week. Each emptied their coin purse on the table, the little pile was cut down the middle and each took half to subsist on till the next payday. It would be many years before Father made the first of his several fortunes.

Father firmly believed and often said that women and children exist to be spoiled. However, it was not easy for him to put his axiom into practice given Mother's penny-pinching. He bought her an endless supply of Swiss lace handkerchiefs which she invariably lost the first day she used them. Once he could afford it, he started buying her precious stones over her protests. He was delighted whenever she could bring herself to spend money on luxuries. He took her to a Czech glass exhibition and, uncharacteristically, she bought several exquisite and expensive pieces including a signed art deco decanter. Many years later, I was charged with its safe delivery when Father moved out to an apartment. I carried it wrapped in a towel on my lap, the stopper in a separate package. Trying to tidy up the apartment before he got there, I yanked at a parcel sitting on the floor. It was the stopper and it now lay in two pieces. Never have I felt so heart sick in my entire life. When Father saw it, he said, "Take it away. Use it to store vinegar." It is the only possession of Father's that I have with me.

Shopping with Mother was an agony. She could spend entire days in a shop without making up her mind. But Father would hang about patiently. Frequently, she would narrow down the choice to two or three items. Father had a way of closing the deal which was quite unique. "Which one do you like the best?" he would ask her. She would tentatively indicate one murmuring, "but..." "All right," Father would jump in, "we'll buy that because it's your pick and this one because it's mine and the third will be useful sometime in the future." And so they would return home with three parcels. Then, ungratefully, Mother would start her criticism. "You railroaded me into buying this; it's the wrong color, it looked different under the lights in the shop; it won't wear well, besides..." We could see a fight in the making and quickly made ourselves scarce.

Father had much success spoiling us. We had only to say we liked something and he would immediately get it for us. He bought ice-cream after school and special gifts to encourage our interests and talents. As we grew older, he gave us jewelry for our dowries. But he did not limit his spoiling merely to what money could buy. He did a lot of little things for his children that I know other fathers did not consider their jobs. They ranged from sitting up with us all night while we toiled for an exam, to checking our hair for dampness every ten minutes after a wash as we sat on the terrace with the drying laundry in the hot blinding sun. It was he and not Mother who applied the awful smelling DDT when we caught lice at school and painted our throats when we caught whooping cough. He was the one who supervised and helped with homework although it was Mother who had been the schoolteacher. During the monsoons he carried each child directly from the car into the building so our shoes would stay dry. He did this even when I was in high school. I still tend to look up expectantly at my escort whenever confronted by a puddle. He made sure there were no mosquitoes lurking inside the net when we went to bed. He soothed us after nightmares. However, he did not tell us bedtime stories. He knew only one about a jackal and an ass which was rather boring. But he would play the violin and mandolin for us if he were in a good mood.

Most of all, he was there to answer an endless stream of questions from morning till night, stand between us and Mother's arbitrary demands, or do for us whatever needed to be done, from ironing our uniforms to teaching us prayers in preparation for our initiation. It was this willing physical and emotional availability of his which was for me the ultimate pampering. It has made me intolerant of men who claim that their work leaves them no time for women and children, or intellectuals whose mental labors leave them unfit for the mundane demands of daily living.

I loved my father because he could be one of us. Mother accused him of buying toys just so he could play with them. But he would spiritedly join us in any game. He let us ride on his back and whirled us around by our arms. He patiently turned our skipping rope and pushed the swing without complaining. When we asked for a bicycle he bought us a shiny Phillips which was then the state of the art. He held onto its back fender as we made our wobbly way round and round the terrace or living room and ran behind it as we tested it out on the slope of Pali Hill. He was perfectly willing to help stick our collection of stamps in an album. And we spent many delightful hours soaking transfers and watching the gorgeously printed butterflies and flowers reappear magically in our scrap book. In first grade he helped me draw fruits and vegetables alongside a vocabulary list and was incensed when the teacher returned the book annotated, "Not your work," next to our perfect peaches and apples.

He did not mind when we played a trick on him. For a short time my brother and I nicknamed him "The Black Rat," perhaps picking up words from abuse hurled at him by Mother. From there it was but a short step to promote him to "King of Black Rats." We decided the occasion called for an installation ceremony. So one afternoon we threw a colorful *sari* from the rag trunk over a broken down wicker chair. When Father came home we eagerly grabbed his arms and led him to the chair. As soon as he sat down, it collapsed and he with it. We could not stop laughing as we told him he had passed the test and he could keep his throne. He assured us he liked being king. In his turn he would tease us by repeating our mispronunciations or lunging at us with an imaginary rapier while uttering a blood-curdling "away with thee to the deepest dungeon beneath the castle walls!" He mimicked people: children asking to be given a ride to a non-existent school, maiden aunts vilifying servants, strangers he had provoked into a display of temper, even our schoolteachers.

Mother strongly disapproved. She never joined in our work or play. When I once asked her to help me with embroidery required for school, she demanded, "Who is going to get a grade for this work?" "I am," I said naively. "Then you should be the one doing it," she declared, flinging the wretched material across the floor. I never went to her for help with anything ever again.

Before the beginning of each school year, Father spent a weekend covering all our text and notebooks. From the mills he would bring home extra heavy brown paper, glazed on one side, its rag lines faintly showing through in a pin-stripe effect. The book to be covered was laid open on the paper which was cut leaving a two inch wide margin all around. Next, the margins on the two long sides were folded in over the book cover. Then an apex-less triangle was cut the exact width of the spine. Finally, the top and bottom strips were turned in after folding their corners at a 45 degree angle. Neither rain, nor spilled ink, nor a sandwich squashed accidentally in the school bag could stain our books after that. On the fly leaf, Father wrote our names in his perfect Roman script and on the top of page twenty-one he inscribed our initials as an anti-theft device.

It gave me great pleasure as a child to watch my Father's quick and clever fingers at various tasks. I observed him every morning rolling up his shirt sleeves. First, he extended his left arm slightly bent. Then, with a deft flick of his right wrist, he made the initial fold the same width as the cuff. Three more flicks and the sleeve lay flat and unrebellious at the elbow. The whole procedure was then repeated with the other arm.

He concentrated mightily on whatever he was doing even if it was merely sharpening a pencil. His eyes would narrow, the tip of his tongue would be clenched between his teeth as he rolled the pencil under a steady penknife in order to notch a clean, straight line all around its girth. Then the sudden smell of freshly shaved wood as soft curls of it fell away under the long upward strokes of the knife. Finally, resting the newly revealed lead on a piece of paper, he honed it to a sharp point leaving behind a fine tracery of graphite.

The way he flipped out the tongues of our shoes when he polished them, the deftness with which he held the pleats of Mother's *sari* to align them at her feet, the economy of gesture with which he cut a mango into squares and triangles, have made me critical of other men's handiwork.

I have also acquired from him a love for beautiful tools and the desire to bestow meticulous attention on their spit and polish. Father owned a collection of pens with a variety of nibs, each for a special purpose. There was one for signing report cards, another for addressing gift envelopes in red ink, yet another to be handed to a child on exam day. They were all kept upright in a jar on the second shelf of his cupboard together with the compartmentalized coin box, the flashlight and the spare pair of eyeglasses. He had Shaeffers with solid gold caps and Parkers with their arrowed haloes over the name. There were a few we were not allowed to use, like the Mont Blanc, for fear of spoiling the angle on the nib. And then there was a translucent grey Pelican which I borrowed and lost the first week of school. I went to every pen shop in town starting with the little hole in the wall he patronized at Flora Fountain, but I never found a duplicate.

I think it was this admiration for something well made, of form conforming to function, that made him so proud and possessive of the Morris. It was a 1948 six-cylinder English car, a very fast one for its time. Its gleaming black paint, unique body lines, and leather interior satisfied his sense of opulence. He could not bear to let chauffeurs drive it, and they sat wincing next to him as he cut and thrust through traffic. It responded to his handling like a thoroughbred. Its engine had a distinctive high pitched whirr which allowed us to hear Father's arrival long before we saw the elongated bonnet turn in the driveway. It had curious decorative turn signals like little illuminated flags on foot long poles attached to the front fenders. These proved irresistible to street urchins who snapped them off whenever the car was left unattended on a city street. Father's pain and anger grew with each successive missing lamp until, in a fit of ire, he had them removed permanently. But this was the only alteration he allowed to be made. Every missing part, screw or bolt was immediately replaced, every nick and scratch was attended to at once, every squeak and rattle silenced without delay, and such extravagant attention was lavished over two decades.

Father had evolved a whole set of rules of the road that had nothing to do with any official doctrine. He would walk around the car before starting to make sure a child was not squatting close to the wheels admiring itself in the chrome hubcaps. He would slow down for children and animals, but not for other traffic, and taxis in his way drove him into a frenzy of maneuvering to get ahead. Father never blew his horn at animals. "It confuses them," he said, "and they are as likely to charge the car as to move out of the way," although I have never seen such wanton violence by any four-footed creature. Instead, Father would race the engine ever so slightly to warn the shepherd and quicken the pace of his charges. He was much less considerate with pedestrians strolling in the middle of the street. He would reach out and slap them soundly on the back as he wheeled around them.

The Morris cut so dashing a picture and was driven with such panache by Father that traffic rules were suspended for him. Policemen on traffic duty could not possibly halt him. Even those not on Father's *bakshish* list briskly and abruptly changed the signal when they saw the Morris approaching an intersection, leaving the cursing taxi drivers to come to a screeching halt on the cross road.

Father did not have friends. He had legions of minions to order around since their caste and class inferiority made them his dependents. With his own superiors he was deferential but aloof. With his equals he invariably quarreled. Even those who genuinely liked him gave up attempts at friendship after a few years of the tantrums and bullying he put them through.

He did, however, inspire doglike devotion from most of his immediate subordinates. One of these was never heard to utter a word even in greeting. He merely raised a padded paw and bestowed a pontifical blessing with a sickly smile. Another was "S" who was an ally, a confidant, employee, foot soldier and general factotum. "S" gave himself unstintingly to Father from the day the two met at the textile mills to the day "S" died almost three decades later.

"S" was a traditional Parsi garbed in the traditional *dagla* and *fenta* and employed at the traditional Parsi occupation of accounting clerk. He referred to Father as "Boss" and echoed the last half of every sentence Father uttered. Thus:

Father: "These Congresswallas are all swines and bastards and ruining the country."

"S": "Yes, ruining it."

Father: "They should be kicked out of office."

"S": "Right out of office."

Father: "Even my own children don't listen to me anymore!"

"S": "No, children don't listen."

Father: "Well, S, it just isn't like it used to be."

"S": "No, Boss, it just isn't like it used to be."

For the first fifteen years of their acquaintance, "S" covered for Father at the mills when, grandly, Father would drive off in the Morris for an afternoon rendezvous. For the next fifteen years, after Father started his own manufacturing firm, "S" caught the express from Parel to Andheri at the end of the day at the mills, arriving on the stroke of five at Father's factory. He had no particular title nor any specific duties assigned to him. He merely walked around the shop floor and fixed any worker who was not producing at the prescribed rate with the glare of a slightly enraged hawk. It always worked better than Father's blood-curdling oaths.

Distributed in the various pockets of his modest white *dagla*, "S" carried a thousand rupees in new bank notes at all times, in case Father needed a loan in an emergency. In his desk at the mills, between the payroll and the time cards, he kept a supply of Father's favorite butter biscuits to be produced for tea breaks. During examination week he made sure Father came home with a fresh supply of Staedler pencils all neatly sharpened. On grand family occasions, when Father's high strung nerves led to chains of explosions, "S" followed, two steps behind him, like a dutiful Indian wife, repeating his sentences and producing objects—pen, paper, change, safety pin—as the need arose. On special ceremonial occasions like *navjots* "S" was the bagman collecting and meticulously recording gifts given by guests whilst keeping an eye on the caterer's count. During hospital stays, especially if it involved one of the children, he was the evening relief guard. During the divorce case he was the silent witness to the entire drama.

Once, when a mechanic impounded the Morris over a dispute regarding payment, Father decided to retrieve it himself on a dark night. At midnight "S" arrived at the house. "Boss, I've got everything: candles, matches, spare keys, wire cutters and I've a taxi waiting to take us there." "Perfect, "S", but I'll go by myself," said Father. "But, Boss," said "S" in a firm voice, "you will need someone to hold the candle!" I never once heard my imperious father give "S" a direct order.

Father rewarded loyalty handsomely. He tipped his barber twice the cost of the haircut. The fishwife who saved the plumpest and freshest of her catch for him got a prince's ransom for her trouble. He paid off the gambling debts of his houseboy, who I think still works for Father. Father's factory workers sought his advice on their wives' barrenness, their sons' waywardness and their daughters' marriages. For their benefit, he played financier, psychiatrist, medical officer, labor leader, father confessor, and not infrequently, God, although he modestly claimed to be merely "the younger brother of God." As for "S", Father helped him with his family's problems, amongst them his sister's insanity and his brother's profligacy.

Father had a prodigious memory and knew the name of every worker at every machine in the dyeing and printing department. He remembered which of his workers had a tubercular child and which a problem mother-in-law, and quietly did what he could to help.

Most of the time, however, Father dealt with the world through intimidation. Physical violence against those weaker or inferior to himself is a male's prerogative in Indian society. It is through threats and actual violence that caste hierarchy is maintained in a village and a man's authority upheld in the home. But Father was exceptionally prone to making his point with his fists. Although short, he developed tremendous strength and I have seen him fell a man twice his size with one blow. He cultivated a mean looking moustache which in later years he grew long, curling the ends upwards with wax, which made him look like a tin-pot dictator. He also developed a permanently belligerent stance towards the world. He usually carried a knuckle-duster in his pocket to do a thorough job, but I don't think he ever used the revolver in the glove compartment.

Neither Mother nor the children were exempt from his violent temper. I avoided physical punishment by an appearance of scrupulous adherence to his rules but the other three were not so astute or lucky. Father purchased the long feather dusters sold by itinerant peddlers at traffic lights in the city. The duster was ostensibly to get the cobwebs off the high chandeliers, but I never saw it used for this purpose. It was made of dyed chicken feathers glued to a long flexible cane. Father would grasp the feathered end and use the other to whip a miscreant, shedding a rainbow of feathers. When one of these got broken, usually on my brother's legs, it would be immediately replaced by an even more resplendent one.

In retrospect, none of us deserved physical punishment. At school our teacher held us up as examples of good behavior. We won awards for obedience and perfect attendance. We were being punished at home simply for being children. Dumping clothes inside-out in the wash basket, leaving a toothbrush on the sink instead of in its holder, losing a pen or a color-box at school, talking even in whispers when Father was trying to nap, befriending a child who happened to belong to the wrong family—any of these could occasion a caning. My brother was constantly, harshly beaten for teasing or beating one of his sisters and Father's outbursts of violence against my mother could be provoked by nothing at all. In her turn, she vented her anger and frustration on us, but we could always outrun her.

My parents quarreled every day about everything. The most innocuous comment, the slightest gesture could blow up into a major battle with enough blood and gore to warrant medical attention. I have seen my parents fight over which child should be sent to take a bath first. I have seen them draw blood over the selection of a pair of shoes. I have watched them sit down to a game of Bezique and, even before the hand had been dealt, the room would be thick with accusations and suddenly cards and vases and eyeglasses would be sailing through the air. I have observed a festive meal that started with blazing chandeliers and waltzes, end with rice on the floors, and plates scattered in countless fragments. A Strauss waltz still makes me queasy. Each outburst involved an almost ritual recitation of all previous battles to date.

I will never forget the fracas that occurred on the day we went to the Russian circus. Father had paid scalpers an exorbitant amount for the best seats, because Mother couldn't decide till the very last minute whether she wanted to go or not.

We start late, and Father's fast driving on the way elicits a running commentary from Mother in the back seat. When we reach the red and white striped tent we have to climb over people's feet to be seated which makes Father squirm with embarrassment. Half an hour into the show the youngest starts to whimper, demanding to go to the bathroom. Mother orders me to take her. The portable loos are a very long way off from the tent, and Father thinks it unfair to make me miss several eye-popping acts involving the Siberian tigers. So he demands that Mother herself escort the child; at which point Mother's nerves snap, and her voice starts to rise. She reaches over and pinches my arm hard, and starts to scold me loudly for not obeying her immediately and thereby giving Father a chance to object. Unable to take any more, Father yanks two of the kids by the arms and starts towards the exit. Mother follows, furious, the other two beginning to snivel behind her. The sorry procession marches to the car to an accompaniment of escalating accusation and counter-accusation.

Father, beside himself with rage, lashes out at anyone within reach. As he starts homeward, Mother begins her standard lament and the children cry about missing the elephants and bears, not to mention the fabled tigers. As the car reaches Marine Drive, Mother, declaring her intention to throw herself into the wind-whipped Arabian Sea, flings open the door on her side. Father swerves onto the grass median but before the car can come to a halt she jumps out and runs through the traffic to the sea wall. We follow, weeping and pleading at the top of our voices, asking her to desist, at least till we are older, before she ends it all. Mother sits on the high parapet, her legs dangling over the black rocks way below. Then, as a sudden frugal impulse strikes her, she starts stripping her jewelry as we clutch at whatever part of her anatomy we can reach. With jerky movements she wrenches off her emerald ring, the very first expensive gift she had received from Father. Predictably she drops it. There is a sudden shocked silence as the enormity of the loss sinks in. Mother seems to deflate physically as we all crane to follow the ring's trajectory. By now it is close to midnight. After memorizing the exact location (five feet from the third lamp-post after the curve in the road), Father drives his subdued bunch home. Immediately he goes back, armed with Petromax lamps, accompanied by three trusted workers from the nightshift at the mills, to search for the missing ring. With incredible luck he finds it nestled on a rock ledge right below where Mother had perched. He returns at dawn and first pretends he hasn't found it. As Mother blanches, he whips it out of his pocket. She thanks him, and slipping it back on her finger she starts up: "If you would only stay out of my business, none of this would happen..." Exhausted, we dive into the protection of the mosquito curtains and feign sleep.

Even now, I do not know what drove my parents to those orgiastic frenzies. As individuals, although cantankerous, each was intelligent, rational and even compassionate. But the combination seemed to be fatal. Perhaps each saw in the other his own worst self. In a reflective moment, I sadly told my Mother's lawyer that each of my parents would have been much happier married to someone else. "No," he said, with absolute conviction, "there would then have been not two but four miserable people."

In spite of nearly killing each other over the merest trivialities, they seemed to have a powerful attraction between them. We felt bewildered and betrayed when, after having stood between them at great peril to our own life and limb, we watched them retreat together into Mother's bedroom. Even these encounters, not unlike every other interaction between them, frequently ended in bloodshed at three in the morning. Father once tried to explain the incongruity by saying that a man and his wife are like the blades of a scissor; they go in opposite directions from each other at all time but shred anything that comes between them. The logic of this metaphor escaped me totally.

Each child adopted a different strategy to survive this mayhem. Mine was to make myself as inconspicuous as possible and to disappear behind a book while being vigilant for the slightest whiff of trouble in the voices of my parents. I still retain the ability to read the most complex text and yet follow every conversation in the room. My brother took to extravagance in behavior as a defence while the youngest took to the roof of the house, literally, and turned her attention and affections to the stray animals on the estate. She nursed dogs that threw up on her school uniform, played with cobras that danced for her while she clapped in time, and befriended mice for whom she stole rice from the big bin under the kitchen table. Only the middle one did not develop any armor, and became hysterical with pain and fright every time my parents fought. She goes through life, even as an adult, being buffeted by the world.

Watching our parents' destructive behavior has also made it difficult for us to deal with our own angers. We tend to turn them against ourselves. Anger makes me shed pounds faster than starvation. My brother routinely puts himself in incredible physical danger. Only the youngest is capable of calculated rage which she reserves for lazy servants and rabid dogs.

When my parents finally took their differences to court, both engaged a whole gaggle of counselors, solicitors and advocates. These jurists quoted their fees in guineas and were always rushing off to chambers. I think we preferred our mother's because they were more colorful and she took us to visit them frequently so we might vouch for the veracity of her statements. Our presence, however, greatly disturbed the worthies. The most eminent of the lot was her Senior Counsel, a tall, gaunt pillar of the community. He was a survival from the Victorian age which lasted much longer out in the Empire than it did at home. He wore a high collar, like Kipling's, with starched points turned down, the tall Parsi hat and his black gown which he had a habit of flicking behind his back, giving the impression of readying himself for take-off. I was startled to hear him referring to "one of my devils" whom I later discovered to be an apprentice law graduate. He was in fact a caring and courteous old gentleman of great authority towards whom Mother was deferential and on whose orders she actually kept quiet. I think when he lost the case thanks to her courtroom histrionics, he refused to bill her for his services.

The solicitor was a gold medalist at the bar examination and cleverness in man or beast always impressed Mother. She was rather fond of him even though he frequently lost his temper with her. His firm's offices were in an ornate old building, an ex-palace in fact, which was located close to my college. So it fell to me to hand-deliver to him Mother's weekly instructions and briefs in her spidery hand on long foolscap paper. Since he was usually in court all day, I had to wait for several hours after college to see him. Late in the evening I would trudge over the cricket pitch of the Oval and through the dust of the Cross Maidan dreading the interview. To lessen my distress, he would order tea. A *chaprasi* in uniform and dusky knees served it in the firm's massive silver set. The solicitor would gravely pour me a cup and thank me for Mother's tattered notes. As I forced myself through the recitation of her "instructions" he would pretend not to notice my stuttering delivery or my closeness to tears. After a few sessions of this sort, he helped me out of the intolerable situation by saying on my arrival, "I know what your mother wants me to do. Now, what's that book you are reading?" We would then spend a happy hour or so chatting about history, politics and the latest good reads. When I got home, Mother would demand a verbatim report of the interview. I could not possibly tell her I had spent the evening with her lawyer discussing the causes of the Reformation or debating the merits of Thackeray!

Later in the battle, Mother was represented by a woman advocate who had been her student in high school. That one regaled us with stories of how as a teacher Mother had had the same terrible temper and recited poetry to the class with such verve that she practically tossed the words out through the window. This lady was of intimidating size, had an abrasive courtroom style, and had earned a reputation for saving the necks of murderers. She proudly told us that when she went to meet her clients in jail they would offer her pots of money with the plea, "Only Allah upstairs and your Ladyship downstairs can save me."

Mother's second solicitor was a very short, balding man whom we nicknamed "Lizard" from his habit of pulling his neck into his body and his body into his vast leather chair in an intransigent pose. Late in life he had married a good looking, well educated, much younger woman who appeared to be very happy at having married him. Mother took this to imply virtues in the man that were certainly not apparent from his exterior. He earned the undying contempt of my youngest sister because, when she told him she would not obey a court order sending her to boarding school, he dismissed the possibility with a dart of his tongue and the word "unthinkable" repeated thrice.

Father's lawyers were all uniformly mean looking and delighted to have for a client a man with seemingly unlimited resources. We spent several eternities in the grimy, pigeon-filled corridors of the High Court as these men negotiated our fate behind closed doors.

I tried to cling to sanity through this awful period by concentrating on my studies. I was determined to excel at the exams and spent hours in the college library learning entire paragraphs by heart from the great English historians. Gibbon, Macaulay, Trevelyan, Churchill, all were acquired effortlessly in the company of a wonderfully patient classmate of my brother's who became my friend and confidant at this time. He was pointed out to me as he was crossing the college quadrangle and I was immediately taken by his unselfconscious good looks. To my great surprise he found me pretty and stopped by between classes to chat with me. He was a dreamer with a perpetually bemused air and a habit of drifting off into the latest hit song from the Hindi films. As I recited my catalog of woes to him, he toyed with my braids and hummed absent-mindedly. But he did laugh at my jokes and showered me with an easy affection that sustained me through the death throes of my parents' marriage.

They had defied the world in order to get married. Now each was looking for absolution from society for that original sin. During the trial Father put on a miserably wronged or a sweetly rational mien by turns. Mother made ringing demands for "Justice." Since she refused to specify damages, would a public flogging appease her desire for retaliation? asked the judge sarcastically. The butcher, the baker, and the Irani restaurateur in the jury box grinned in appreciation of this witticism. And so it went on for twenty-eight days.

I was absent from the climax of this blood-letting. The prospect of testifying against my father was so humiliating that I attempted suicide. I was found a few hours later and rushed to the hospital where I remained until after the verdict. Mother construed my action as inherent selfishness and saw in it one more proof of my disloyalty to her cause. This thirteen year melodrama that was my parents' divorce case was brought to its end only by the death of Mother just one day before her appeal to the highest court in the land.

FIVE

Mountains are delightful
only at a distance

— Gujarati proverb

It is customary for middle-class urban Indians living in the hot plains to retreat to cooler mountain air in the summers. In our family the annual pilgrimage to the hill station was marked by penance before and during the event. My mother would start in March, quoting authorities on the need for bracing mountain air for the proper growth of her fragile children. By April she could point to our oozing, angry boils in support of her argument. By mid-May, after several bouts of plate throwing, she had made her point. A particular hill station from among several in the Western Ghats would be selected for the vacation. It might be Matheran, very popular with Parsis, which could be reached by a toy train from the plains. Or, more frequently, it would be the twin stations of Panchgani and Mahabaleshwar.

The big, black metal trunk would be dusted off. Three changes of clothing per day per child somehow had to be packed into it. But that was only the start. A medical kit adequate to serve a Himalayan expedition was also taken along. And school books so that next year's math exercises and French translations could be worked on during the holiday. Toys and puzzles, umbrellas and walking sticks, all had to be packed and strapped together. The family car, the sturdy Morris, needed some twenty-five days of overhauling before the journey. All kinds of emergency belts, loops, and tow ropes for the car had to be prepared for the 200 mile trip. And this included the raw eggs which Father had read in the "Helpful Hints" section of *Reader's Digest* worked to plug leaks in radiators.

On the previous night, the children were forced to bed at sunset. We had to start off at sunrise in order to avoid traveling in the worst of the heat. This procedure didn't really pay off because both parents paced the house and continuously argued all through the night about the packing.

On the day itself we arose at 4:30 and talked in whispers from the excitement. After much ado about dressing, there would be more about who would sit where in the car. The baby of course went on Mother's lap or sometimes would be neatly laid on the parcel shelf behind the back seat.

Father would make a determined effort to get the expedition off on the right foot by singing "La Paloma" which would quickly be reduced to a "tra la la la la", since he never knew more than the first line of any song. The children were supposed to join in, but Mother's headache silenced everyone before we had even left the city limits. I liked the first few hours of the journey the best. We went through the shantytowns where the tin roofs glowed red in the light of the rising sun. The morning mist veiled their misery, lending them a romantic mirage-like quality. The occasional woman clutching her thin clothes tightly around her against the morning chill; the *bhaya* with his milk cans hanging by coir ropes from a long pole balanced on his shoulders like a giant scale moving at a quick trot; the owner-less cow struggling to her feet in the dust; the local train whistling its way into the city—all these I watched avidly from between my brother and sister where I was placed to keep them apart and avoid bloodshed in the back seat.

As we made our way further from the coast into the heart of the Deccan Plateau the country became browner. Huge black boulders were strewn over the landscape. The main harvest of winter crops was long over by May, but there might be a sudden small patch of green where a peasant was cultivating vegetables. On our return journey, the fields would be green again. We passed villages set at some distance from the road. I had read about rural India in the children's weekly and had heard about the beauty and rhythms of a simple life close to nature. These villages did not impress me and curiously there were very few people. Except for a long line of women with towers of brass water pots on their heads, the teeming millions seemed not to be about. Frequently, these women would stop in single file at the edge of the road to let the traffic pass. I was struck by their patience, their silent waiting. Sometimes we saw a blindfolded camel walking eternally round and round a well, drawing water for the dusty fields.

We could hear some sounds over the purr of the car engine: a creaky water wheel, dogs barking, the braying of a potter's donkey. Mother made Father slow down and even stop so the children could appreciate bird song. There was the shrilling of the drongo, the insistent carrying-on of the brain-fever bird and, always at this time of the year, the cuckoos. Sometimes we had botany lessons by the roadside as Mother pointed out the wild flowers.

We drove with the widows down, but every time a truck was seen approaching from the opposite direction, all hands on deck sprang into action to roll them up to prevent the billows of dust from choking the baby. But trucks were not always a nuisance. Father called truck drivers the true gentlemen of the road. On these one-lane Indian highways, the only way to pass one is with the help and cooperation of the driver ahead who watches out on your behalf for oncoming traffic. Most would also oblige by squeezing their vehicles, gaily painted with auspicious slogans on them, almost into the ditch.

Periodically, the car was stopped to check the luggage strapped to the carrier on top.

When we were younger, we stayed overnight in Poona in order to get a fresh morning start on the long winding climb of the Western Ghats. Poona was a British army cantonment. I remember it as a city of flowers. The Bund Garden near the river was always ablaze with canna, phlox and petunia; each little bungalow came with its orderly borders and ornamental trees. We saw the old Maharani Chimnabai covered in sorrow and pearls driving slowly around the gardens in her black Rolls Royce. When Mother finally got her house with a garden, Father drove all the way to Poona to fetch her English rose cuttings from the best nursery.

The hairpin curves on the mountain road were always problematic. I hear my father chanting the rules at the foot of the ascent: focus your eyes on distant peaks and you won't feel giddy; always blow your horn as you approach a blind curve; pull over to let descending trucks pass; use brake and low gear alternately to prevent brake drums from overheating; and, last but not least, respect the little wayside shrines carved out of the rock face to ensure a safe journey. These local deities at whose shrines all truck drivers threw coins, as we do at toll booths, kept them from harm on their weekly run up these treacherous roads. Neither distant vistas nor deities could, however, prevent car sickness in each child in turn and there would be emergency stops at precarious scenic spots and much horror at the thought of getting one's shoes splashed with that afternoon's lunch.

As we climbed higher, the air would turn cold and all the children would have to put on sweaters kept in an emergency bag inside the car. As darkness descended, the mountain peaks took on threatening shapes, the thick jungle made unfamiliar noises. There was always a quarrel at the top about which way to turn for a short-cut into the town. But somehow we got there.

All Indian hill stations are built to the same plan: a lake, usually man-made, the main shopping street, the mall for evening walks, a cricket pitch, gymkhana, race track, and botanical gardens. Country lanes lead out of town towards "points" which were in fact vantage points with uninterrupted views from which one could survey a particular valley or range. There were cottages and villas dotting the slopes with names like "Sans Souci" and "Bellevue." Mother would wistfully point to some particularly attractive one covered with climbing columbine which she thought would make a good refuge for her brood. After she had died and we children had all left for different parts of the world, Father was inspired to build a vacation bungalow for his family in one of these hill stations.

The long days were filled with long walks, longer drives, boating on the lake and three whole, sit-down meals which were the worst trials of my life. I particularly disliked the lilac colored blanc mange served once a week at the hotel and Mother's constant complaints about the quality and quantity of the food drove everyone to desperation. Father secretly paid twice the boarding charges to ensure special menus but even that could not guarantee that the food would not cool on the long trek through the garden between the kitchen and the dining room, and Mother's wails could be heard as far as the main road.

The other tribulation was the toilets. On our first few visits, modern sanitation had not yet reached the mountains and there were out-houses like pill boxes with a hole in the raised floor and a straw basket below. The cold air would rush up through the floor and the tin door never closed properly. An untouchable *mehtrani* would empty the baskets twice a day. Mother would march up to the management and file complaints about her negligence and dereliction of duty. My father would quietly slip the *mehtrani* a large denomination banknote to do an extra cleaning just before Mother was going to use it. Once, Mother saw him transacting business with the *mehtrani* and promptly accused him of seducing an untouchable.

Occasionally, there were special expeditions to some remote peak or valley which involved requesting a picnic lunch from the hotel. Sometimes it was a trip to a waterfall where wild orchids clung to the damp rocks. At other times it might be a point like Arthur's Seat where a throne-like structure was carved by wind and rain from the granite face of the cliff. It was a four thousand foot drop from the overhang. The point was totally exposed and the deep ravines on both sides created tremendous gusts of wind. We had to clutch the rusty white railing in order not to be blown over. Mother was convinced that Father's playful push on one such visit was meant in deadly earnest.

Once in a while it was the botanical gardens. The one at Mahabaleshwar had groves of eucalyptus trees that scented the air for miles. It also had an apiary where Mother could buy bottles of pure honey for the mixture administered to my youngest sister for her chronic cough. There were experimental nurseries where new breeds were developed. This one had produced a fabled black rose which was in fact a crimson so dark that it verged on black. I thought it rather ugly.

Another thing that hill stations in India are known for are their boarding schools. They were usually run by the Christian missions or Catholic orders. There were a very few run by Parsis. All the children came from unusual circumstances. There were orphans and children of converted Hindus who proved the sincerity of their new found faith by agreeing to educate their children in a truly Christian institution. Others were from wealthy upwardly mobile city families who wished to give their children all the advantages of an English education, and quite a few were the offspring of divorced parents.

Boarding schools are totally against the grain of Indian child raising practices. Young children are indulged and pampered; daughters because they are considered guests of short duration in their natal families, and sons because they alone bestow meaning on their mother's life. On one trip Father decided my brother and I should be sent to boarding school. I was five years old and had completed kindergarten at the Parsi Gujarati-medium school where Mother had been a teacher. My brother was four and had had only that year at the pre-school. A Catholic convent was chosen for me and a Parsi boys' school for him. Mother considered it unnatural to separate her children from her but Father thought it would reduce the burden on her if two of the three could be looked after by someone else. Had not she herself been sent away for years at a stretch to her uncle's home so that her mother could turn her attention to the succession of younger ones? Reluctantly she agreed. Neither child was informed of the decision.

We were taken to the local tailor to be fitted with school uniforms. Mine was a grey cotton pinafore over a white blouse, a long sleeved white silk shirt with a navy serge skirt for Sunday service, and sufficient night clothes and undergarments, all to be embroidered with the number 52 in red thread. I also got my first dressing gown styled just like Mother's. It was a sky blue crêpe de chine scattered with white Monet-like lilies which I wore between the dormitory and the showers once a week. My frugal and far-sighted Mother had our clothes tailored to fit us five years into the future. Consequently, we always wore baggy clothes. My brother's short pants ended below the calf; he shortened them with safety pins to avoid ridicule at school. I still find decently fitting clothes too tight. All the seams were six inches wide and frock hems were ten inches doubled over twice. Skirts that buttoned at the waist had a whole series of buttons which could be used in sequence through the years. The entire garment could be reconstructed to grow with the child. That blue serge skirt fitted me perfectly in my first year in college when pleated skirts came back into fashion.

My parents had made the boarding school decision in a hurry and did not have enough time to provide all that was necessary. I had two very thin, summer pajamas and not enough heavy outer clothes. I was bitterly cold for the entire nine months there.

One bright, sun-filled day I was driven without my brother or sister through a pair of iron gates, down a long drive to a huge red brick structure with pointed roofs. Behind it loomed a cliff locally called the "table-land" since its top was completely flat as if someone had decapitated a mountain cleanly. We walked into the foyer where we were greeted by a curiously dressed individual. I could not tell the sex of the person, for I had not seen a nun before.

She escorted my parents into her office, and I was left standing by myself. Not having been inside an institutional building, I was fascinated by the size of the carved teak staircase. I heard children's voices but could not make out what was being said. Someone was practicing scales on a piano in a remote part of this massive building.

My parents emerged. Father told me that this was where I would go to school from now on. It was called a boarding school, a very good and very expensive one. I was to behave even better than I did at home. Mother gave detailed instructions on how to keep myself clean, cautioned me not to befriend the wrong kind of child. Then they left.

They had failed to explain to me that a boarding school was one where you lived day and night and did not return home in the evenings. They did not tell me that it was an English language school where no one was allowed to speak anything but English, and it had slipped their minds that my knowledge of that language was limited to nouns. They had also forgotten to show me where the toilets were located. I spent the first three days weeping because I desperately needed to use the bathroom. I could not ask for directions since no one understood the vernacular I was speaking. I followed older girls around hoping one of them would end up there. Finally, on the third night I wet the bed. I was punished for it by having to sleep on the floor the next night.

When, years later, I questioned my father about why he had not explained what a boarding school was to a five year old, he exclaimed, "I thought you knew! You were such a clever little girl, I was certain you knew!"

I hated boarding school.

Out of necessity, I learned to speak coherent English in the incredibly short span of a week. Within ten days, the other girls understood what I was saying and I could eavesdrop on their conversations. My father had arranged to have me tutored in the language by a Goanese teacher at the school. I amazed her by teaching myself to read the first story in the reader after only two sessions with her. It was titled "Alladin and His Magic Lamp."

I cannot recall a single face from the horde of children there. I did not know how to make friends. Our parents discouraged us from infancy from social intercourse with anyone outside the immediate family. My father did so because he grew up a friendless child himself and disapproved of anyone different, especially Hindus. He referred to all non-Parsis deprecatingly as "Ghatis," a species of low caste mountain tribals. My mother was worried about us picking up infections from other children or, worse still, head lice or worms. I desperately missed my brother and sister, my only friends, during that boarding school year. The other girls disliked me and I thought their games silly. One favorite game of these homeless children was to draw the outline of a house in stones on the ground and then play house assuming the roles of mother, father and child.

Every Saturday, to get proper exercise, we had to march to the table-land, play organized games up there and walk back in time for dinner. It was a long, steep climb and icy, gusty winds almost blew me down on the treeless waste at the top. My teeth chattered from the cold and I would squat hugging my knees behind the nearest big rock. Since I was too small and too cold to join in any organized game, I was quickly appointed the guardian of the raincoats shed by the players. A girl once found a large tear in hers and accused me of ripping it out of spite. I was so taken aback at the absurdity of her accusation that I did not even defend myself. I think after that incident I gained a reputation for being a jealous, malicious little monster, and the others avoided me even more.

My only act of conscious defiance occurred at prayers. I refused to cross myself after saying grace. I knew instinctively that my parents would not approve of this gesture. At first, an older girl, thinking I was ignorant, would grab my arm and force the performance. After a month, they gave up on me. I went to church every Sunday with the others, and knelt to pray every night, but I would not make the sign of the cross.

The only person I liked there was a Scottish art teacher who befriended me because I showed so little talent at drawing.

Once a week we had to write a letter home. The English teacher wrote it out on the blackboard from where it was copied by thirty diligent little girls. My father still hoards the entire collection he received from me. In later years he often recited the first one aloud from memory, "Dear daddy, This is our national flag," followed by a smudgy drawing with the three colors reversed. Not owning any crayons myself, I had to borrow them, and since all the other girls were using their orange one first to fill in the top panel, I decided to start with the green and finish with the orange so I would not lag behind the class. The letters always signed off with "your loving daughter."

During my nine month confinement, my parents came twice to see me. The first time it was Father with a friend of his who was over six feet tall, unusual for an Indian. He also had gold teeth which I stared at in wonder. He brought me gifts: a pair of pink fluffy bedroom slippers which I never used since I was unsure of what constituted an appropriate occasion to wear them, and a bag, very large, of the best Swiss chocolates which you could get from the confectioners in the city. I was eating my second one when Mother Superior popped into the visiting room. "We don't want a sick little girl, do we?", she asked as she took the bag away from me. I never saw the chocolates again. Father took me out for a walk and a meal.

The second visitor was my mother. She felt uneasy about my health and since my Father would not make the trip with her, she decided to come using the long distance public buses even though she was six months pregnant. Mother's intuition was always correct. I was suffering from jaundice and had been kept in the infirmary for weeks without my parents being notified. I had passed the hours listening to the distant sound of passing cars. I knew it was merely a matter of time before I heard the unmistakable Morris engine. My mother's visit was a relief, but it complicated matters for me. She vehemently accused the nuns of starving and neglecting me. After she left I was put through an hour long grilling about the exact words I had used in my conversation with Mother. I am not sure why she did not just take me home with her.

Three months later, my mother dreamt of four nuns carrying a very small coffin down a flight of stone steps. After that there was no question or doubt I was coming home. Father arrived and I have a photo of me and him on liberation day, standing outside the walls of the convent. I come up to his knee and my pigtails look strange. He always braided them too tightly putting bends in them. He was however quite good at combing out the knots from waist-long hair without painful pulling and jerking the way Mother did.

My brother's boarding school episode lasted a mere forty hours. Since he was so young, the principal thought it wise to let him stay with his own young son rather than in the dormitory. As soon as my parents left his sight, he set up a howl and continued until he had cried himself into a 102° fever. The principal requested my parents to fetch him the next day.

I know my brother missed me terribly that year. The servant reported that on the day of my return he had insisted on crossing the railway bridge on all fours as he walked home from school in order, he said, to get there faster for my arrival. My mother complained that I was no longer her soft-spoken child but had learned to quarrel like a fish-wife. My father was just relieved to have me back in his presence. He said he could not sleep when any of us were out of his sight. Three times each night he made a round of his sleeping children, pulling a blanket over one, straightening the mosquito curtain of another, removing a thumb that might ruin the smile from the mouth of the third. My dreams were lonely without his ministrations when he left us.

Our Navjot

Friends and Family at Navjote

We Visit Elephanta Caves

Parsis Praying: Victoria Station in Background

Father and the Redoubtable Morris

Top: Parsis as They Used To Be
Bottom: Bombay in Father's Childhood

SIX

Why should I bring rice with me
when I go to my elder sister's house?
—Tamil proverb

My parents are fond of repeating a story about how I felt towards my new-born brother who is just thirteen months younger than myself. Whenever I was left alone in the room with the baby, they could hear my voice talking to him only to be punctuated shortly by a scream from him. They found this puzzling, so they hid and watched. As usual, I started talking sweetly to him but in a few moments I reached over and firmly pinched the sole of his foot, returning immediately to the soothing patter. Father also likes to recall that once, when he lost his temper with his colicky son, I said to him, "God gave you a quiet daughter but you were not pleased; so he gave you a howling son. You should be happy."

Even if these stories are true, my jealousy toward my brother must have evaporated very quickly. I remember him as my best playmate. We did everything as one. Mother enjoyed teaching me. She said I was so eager that I was impossible to distract, but my brother required too much effort. So I took over the job of transmitting to him in the afternoon what I had learned from her in the morning. Similarly, when I went off to nursery school for the first time, I would immediately start tutoring him on my return, but now with the aid of my new slate that smelled of sweet earth when washed.

In those long, still afternoons of our childhood when Mother retreated to her four-poster, we stole into the room of the paying guest which was forbidden to us. We climbed onto the vast Victorian bed which we used as a stage to put on dramas of our own devising. Once our parents caught us giving a dance recital in there. That morning Mother had shown us a picture of a *Bharat Natyam* dancer with her gorgeous costume, gold jewelry and wildly gesticulating limbs. At noon we armed ourselves with all the golden tape to be found in the house. Fruit baskets in India arrive tied with this kind of tape. It is flat, has a two-thread-deep red edge and a diamond pattern in the center. My brother and I tied yards of it around our ankles, wrists, necks and a band each around the forehead. We debated how it could be tied through the nose in imitation of the dancer's dangling nose ring but gave the idea up in despair after several tries. Then, together on our stage we contorted our limbs, pointed our toes and rolled our eyes in concert. Suddenly we heard clapping and saw our parents smiling in the doorway. We stopped, abashed, and were shooed out of the room with only a mild scolding.

In the early evening we were allowed to go out for a walk with a servant. We had our favorites. Like the young north Indian fellow who teased Mother and begged her to tune in the radio to a station playing Hindi film songs. He promised to show us a red cow and one evening we set off on a long march to see this wondrous beast. I imagined it to be the color of the sky at sunset, streaked with various shades of fiery pink. After a weary hour we ended in a meadow where a solitary cow stood licking its nostrils. It was brown with white patches. I broke into tears in exasperation and accused the boy of lying. He carried us back in his arms as a consolation. Mother righted things by explaining that in Hindi the word for "brown" is the same as the one for "red." That was my first lesson in the impossibility of translation.

Sometimes when Mother was in a pleasant mood she let us go out unescorted to "make friends," as she put it. We, however, did not join the games of the other children. They were rowdy and pushed and chased each other, which we did not find in the least entertaining. Instead the two of us would try to catch white and blue butterflies in the unmowed grass. Or we would walk all the way across the development to the farthest fence and feel very bold. During these forays outdoors, I was in charge and responsible for the actions of both of us.

One evening, my brother insisted on defying the rule not to step outside the fence by sticking various parts of his body through it to the other side. I warned him several times, but he ignored me. Finally, he managed to force his head through two bars which were slightly out of line. To my horror he cold not pull it back in. Greatly alarmed, I ran around through the gates to the other side and pushed his head with my whole body. Nothing happened. By now he was sobbing. I continued to struggle for a very long time, alternately pulling and pushing him until I was exhausted.

Finally, as the light began to fade, I knew I had no choice but to go tell Mother. When I got home, I casually said to her that my brother's head seemed to have swollen during play. Consequently, I could not bring him back with me. Mother pounced on me and proceeded to shake more information out of an incoherent little girl. She rushed out in her housecoat and on reaching him put my brother through another hour of pushing and pulling. She too was unable to do anything. It was pitch dark before enough men and tools could be gathered to force the bars apart. When I returned home a few years ago, I drove past that fence. Two of its bars still gape wide enough apart to allow a small child to walk through.

I was also responsible for stopping him from eating wall plaster. He must have suffered a calcium deficiency. He would scrape off small bits of the flaking stuff and swallow them. My parents interpreted this behavior not as a medical problem but as a reflection of his perversity. Both of us got punished repeatedly, he for doing it and I for failing to prevent it. His condition must have been acute, because he also ate my entire doll with her plaster of Paris face and limbs. When my sister got her play tea-set plastic had replaced china in toys. The first time we played with it, we filled the tea cups with water. My brother had the clever idea of filling the plates with the forks and spoons from the set which he snapped into bits. Half-way through the tea party he decided it would be more fun if we really did consume our tea and, before we could stop him, he had eaten all the broken plastic. When Mother found out, it was castor oil and a tense twenty-four hours of waiting outside the bathroom door. His plaster habit was finally broken by a brutal tactic suggested by an old servant woman. The lower castes use this method to wean older children who refuse to give up the breast. Whenever he was caught doing it, Mother and the servant would grab him. The woman would hold him down while Mother forced open his mouth and stuffed it with the hottest chillies available. He screamed like a goat being bled, but it cured him within a week.

My brother and I had scarcely any toys in the first few years since Father was only an apprentice with a paltry salary. I owned a china tea set with a blue pattern on it, a doll and a set of multi-colored chips which could be arranged in geometric designs. My brother had only a rag doll with a singularly ugly name, but I always allowed him to play with my things. We preferred making up games anyway. Occasionally, we befriended a stray dog or cat, but it would not last. One day a parrot-seller caught our attention. We beckoned him to the door. He belonged to a bird-seller's caste from Kathiawar. Dressed in a knee length shirt, curious accordian-pleated pajamas and elaborate turban, he carried over his shoulder a dozen cages filled with green birds, all atwitter. We begged Mother to let us have one. She did not really need much persuading as the birds had struck a chord in her rural heart. So we acquired a parrot in a metal cage with bars. It had a perch and a water cup. Mother hung it in the kitchen window because, she explained, "The parrot can see the tree and won't feel homesick." That evening she taught us a poem about a parrot with a black necklet around its throat and ruby red eyes. We were ecstatic. We rushed to tell our neighbors. We waited patiently for hours to watch it tuck its head under its wing. We helped mother feed it chillies and pomegranate seeds. She held out the promise that it might actually talk one day.

One afternoon we decided to give the parrot a bath. We had seen Mother clean the cage by splashing water on it. So we turned the faucet on full blast and held the cage under it. The parrot squawked and dashed about in its confined space but we were determined to get every inch of it properly wet. At the end of half an hour, satisfied with our cleaning, we put it in the sun to dry. Next day it was listless and the day after, Mother found a stiff bird on the floor of the cage. It had died of pneumonia. She was upset and puzzled aloud what could have happened. We did not enlighten her. Sadly, we helped with the burial preparations. She wrapped the bird with a lot of sea-salt in a white cloth. We marched outside and dug a hole under the fragrant thousand-petalled *mogra* bush. We laid the bird in its grave. Mother consoled us by saying that the parrot would like coming back as a white flower the following year.

Most of the time my brother followed my lead. He listened to the stories I made up for him, held my doll while I poured tea for her, and, as my problems with food grew worse, obliged by eating my meals which I passed to him under the table, a mouthful at a time. Since my parents' moods were unpredictable, making a simple request could be hazardous. He always acted as my proxy and would dutifully ask Mother which dress I should wear to play in or whether I might be allowed to leave the table. I held his hands for hours to stop him scratching himself bloody with prickly heat and praised his drawings which were always very good. I helped him understand numbers, he polished my essays for school. When he was seven years old, he developed an intense fear of darkness. Every night after our parents had retired, he would creep over to me and beg to be allowed to sleep across the foot of my bed. But the moment I let him, he would want to talk and I could not risk a visit from a parent. So I invented a game, "Tell me, what can you see in the dark?" and when he hesitated, I would prompt, "Witches? Gnomes?. . ." "Devils, demons," he would complete, supplying descriptions from his overwrought imagination, scaring himself thoroughly. Then I would change tactics and insist he was seeing angels and fairies in a garden. Confused, he would ask which was real. Triumphantly, I would demarcate the realms: if he faced the bathroom, he would encounter all that was horrid; if he faced the balcony and the sea, he would be allowed to play in the garden. Studiously, he would turn his face to the ocean and, in his desire to capture the beautiful, forget to chatter.

My brother is an extremely fine mimic, and even Mother would laugh at his imitations of friends and relatives whose eccentric mannerisms are a hallmark of the entire community. However, it was not mere mockery or play acting. He became the half-potted spinster denigrating all men, the big-breasted film star with swishing hips and provocative smile, the servant girl with flailing arms and preposterous excuses. So uncanny would be the transformation that Mother's amusement would turn to unease and the charade would end with her throwing her shoe at him to break the spell.

At school this talent of his was capitalized on by his teachers who gave him starring roles in every play. In kindergarten, being a fair-skinned, large-eyed child gave him an advantage over the rest of his classmates. In his first role, he was cast as a butterfly which allowed him to be transformed into something not even human. He was supposed to flit from flower to flower, played by little girls, and suck the nectar. He repaid his teacher's confidence by biting the flowers viciously on stage since they could neither cry out nor hit him.

Then he got the lead as Gandhi. India had recently gained independence, Gandhi had become a martyred saint and the teachers, groping for a new identity as Indian citizens, put on patriotic plays.

My brother was dressed in nothing but a white loin cloth which the teacher decided needed securing with a good, strong British safety pin. Only she pinned it to his skin. So eager was he to perform, that he said not a word, perhaps he did not even feel it. At the end of the three-hour performance, he was released from a blood soaked costume as he let himself cry with pain.

When he entered an all boys' school, his soft features, fair hair and frail body earned him all the female roles. He got to play the coy daughter of a fat classmate in a Parsi melodrama, Mary in the enactment of the nativity at Christmas, a limp rag-doll of indeterminate sex carried on stage by his favorite male teacher in the fancy dress competition. He won prizes for his performances but it left my parents feeling ambiguous. Father swore he would shoot the drama teacher who had turned his only son into a sissy. When he graduated from acting to directing in college, Father was much more supportive. He paid for the props and even hired a horse drawn buggy to haul the stage scenery to the theatre. My brother does not act in plays any longer. He merely lives out his life as if he were on stage.

I remember the day that our perfect existence came to an abrupt end. It was the day Mother returned home with our younger sister and I lost my dearest playmate. The newcomer was the most beautiful baby I have ever seen. She was a perfectly placid child for the first year of her life, but then she suffered an attack of measles. According to Mother, that permanently changed her personality.

My brother and I were both put to work looking after the baby and we could not retreat into our secret world any longer. She had become an interloper in Paradise. And we did everything to keep her out. When she was old enough to play with us, we pretended to find physical deformities in her which would prevent her from entering into our private realm. Her nails bitten to the quick, the mosquito bites on her legs, the wart on her thumb, these were the disqualifying stigmata. After her birth, Father suddenly started making a lot of money. He was convinced that the newborn girl was his Laxmi, his own goddess of wealth. He showered her with toys; blue-eyed dolls larger than herself, stuffed bears that moved and shook their head from side to side, yellow plastic hens that laid white plastic eggs, tea sets, dinner sets, there was no end to it. She would not let us play with them and after a few days her curiosity would get the better of her. She would smash the toy to see its insides. Father always replaced them immediately.

My brother made her existence miserable. He quarreled with her constantly as he had never done with me. My parents had to continually break up their fights which, as time progressed, became bloodier. In self defence, she became pugnacious and stubborn. The birth of the fourth and youngest merely made matters worse. My brother was overwhelmed with three sisters whose femaleness increasingly confused him. My sister lost her pampered position as the youngest. I was overburdened with the responsibility of keeping three siblings amused and out of trouble.

With adulthood, my brother and I have recaptured our special world. Through time we have grown to be mirror images of each other. I feel with my head, he thinks with his heart. I protect myself with silence, he with a torrent of words. I withdraw in anger, he dashes himself to pieces against the object of his rage. I seek refuge from the world, he engagement. We understand each other without words, without looks, without even being on the same continent. Our cravings and passions coincide. Walking through a glass factory in Murano, I ask him "Which do you like best?" "The square one with diagonal line," we say together and laugh aloud at the identity of taste and desires. We are jealous of each other's friends and lovers. I do not relish his flirtations with death. But, like the Indian dancer twirling bare-footed on the cutting edge of swords, his is a virtuoso performance which makes only the observer's heart stop. He does not approve of my pursuit of security but he boasts of my achievements to all.

There is a photograph of us taken when we were very young. I am standing half a pace ahead of him, feet planted squarely apart, his hand firmly in mine, glaring at the camera. His face is turned up to mine with a half smile. I shall never love anyone with the fierce protectiveness with which I love my brother.

SEVEN

God's stick makes no sound

— Parsi proverb

The one problem that did not trouble us as children was the problem of identity. We knew from the day we understood the spoken word that we were Parsis and therefore different from everyone else around us. What did that mean? First and foremost it meant an awareness of our unique religious heritage. An accident of history had made us a small group of Persian survivors on Indian soil. Religious refugees, fourteen hundred years ago, from the fires and swords of a zealously crusading Islam, we had come here to protect and practice our distinct creed. We were different because we worshipped the fire and honored the prophet Zoroaster. In our own home we had his picture on the living-room wall — a vacant-looking man with soft brown curls and Greek features supporting a golden radiance around his head.

At the local fire-temple there was a full portrait of him in glass. Here he was flanked by two Assyrian winged bulls and had one finger pointing heavenwards. The other hand held a stick with nine nodes, with which he reminded us of God's justice which may be slow and silent but is never capricious. Our parents told us that it was Zoroaster who had brought the message that we should fight with the good Ahura Mazda against the evil Ahriman. Ahura Mazda liked children, Truth, and laughter; Ahriman caused chicken-pox, quarrels, and demons. On certain days we children were taken to the fire-temple. It was a stone building with a notice on the railings in English, "Non-Parsis Not Admitted".

The temple was cavernous and dark. Its large chandeliers were entombed in red cloth bags. In the center presided the eternal sacred fire. The fire for a new temple is always borrowed from an existing one. The first one had to be put together from cinders taken from the hearth of every home from the humblest to the wealthiest, to which was added God's own fire in the form of lightning that a powerful priest could call down from the heavens. Old men and women, their heads covered with funny caps or white cloths, stood in front of the magical sweet-smelling flames, swaying and muttering in sing-song pitches.

We pretended to pray too by humming or turning the pages of the prayer-book. We imitated our parents' gestures, carefully touching our heads to the marble threshold of the room that contained the fire in a huge silver urn. But soon we would be overcome by the heat and the heavy fumes of sandalwood and myrrh. It was a great relief to see the priest in his flouncy dress emerge from the inner sanctum, his mouth covered by a muslin mask. He would extend a silver ladle full of the sacred ashes. Each child was allowed to offer Ahura Mazda one stick of fragrant wood with one silver coin in exchange for a pinch of the ashes. Father would pay the priest to offer a *tandarosti*, a special prayer of health for his family. On the way home Mother would criticize the efficacy of such gestures. Father would try to placate her by saying it was all for the greater glory of God.

All Parsi children have the good fortune to enlist as Ahura Mazda's foot soldiers through the ceremony of *navjot*. It is an initiation rite performed around the age of seven that puts a seal of difference on the Parsi child. I remember the months of hectic preparation and arguments that went into ours. Almost a year in advance Father started teaching us the necessary prayers. That involved memorizing a string of words in Avestan, a long-dead Middle Eastern language, not a bit of whose vocabulary corresponded with those of any of the languages we spoke. Father would try to spark our interest by reading aloud the translations into Gujarati that appeared at the end of the prayer-book. This did not aid our understanding at all, but I was hypnotized by the sounds: the sonorous list of the hundred-and-one names of God — *gar-a-gar,* "the transformer of water to fire", *a-gar-a-gar,* "transmuter of earth to fire." I walked around the house making these pleasurable gurgling sounds as soon as I had mastered them.

Mother's old aunt and her daughter came from their little village and stayed to supervise the proceedings. Grandfather would be one of the officiating priests. The day for the ceremony was carefully selected to fall on an auspicious day of the calendar and to avoid the impure states of all the women of the family. To make up for the lack of fanfare at his marriage Father was determined to make the *navjot* of his two oldest children a memorable event. There would be the best caterer with a mile-long menu; an eighteen-piece orchestra to play waltzes and foxtrots. The florist was commanded to build a backdrop of the rising sun out of roses, tube lilies and carnations on the stage where the ceremony was to be performed. And there were ornate garlands for everyone and everything, including the car and the entrance-gate of the house.

On the day of the *navjot* all of Father's friends who owned motor-cars lent them to the family to ferry the guests from the house to the ceremonial garden. I travelled in a huge 1930s Hudson, and was barely able to see out of the window. As usual, we were late because Mother couldn't decide what to wear. When we got there both my brother and I were purified by being bathed in milk and rose petals. My skin felt unfamiliarly slippery after that washing.

And to purify our spirits we were made to sip the sanctified urine of a white bull. This is no common old farmyard bull; it cannot have a single black hair, and it lives in the fire-temple compound where the priests feed it a special porridge laced with butter and sugar. These pampered creatures can grow to be quite vicious and one of them had gored my grandfather in his old age. Mother had prepared us for this trial by assuring us of the medicinal value of uric acid and had added that my brother's eczema might be helped immeasurably. She made it sound so plausible that the poor child eagerly gulped down a whole goblet of the atrocious stuff. After the bath, dressed in white pajamas, our bodies wrapped in beautifully embroidered Kashmiri shawls, we walked in new red velvet slippers to the stage. During the ceremony my brother in his excitement started shouting the prayers in the wrong order. My shawl kept slipping off my greasy shoulders.

But it was all over soon enough, and there we were, two newly minted Zoroastrians being showered with rice and flowers and kissed and blessed by an army of relatives we had never before seen. It being an era of Prohibition, the male guests retreated with Father behind the bath-house to drink to the health of the family and sing the Parsi anthem, "We Are Zoroastrians All!" The women settled down to match-making and criticizing each other.

For a few weeks after the *navjot* we were both models of piety, performing the ritual endlessly before and after meals, after answering each call of nature, and at bedtime. But our new-found religiosity petered out rapidly and soon we had to be reminded every night to say our prayers.

Our *navjot* was only the beginning of a whole lifetime of being a Zoroastrian. We were told that now we were to be incapable of telling lies, however white, or walking away from someone else's need, however trivial, or cheating, however great the temptation. Such acts would not merely be violations of a code, they were tantamount to a violation of our essence. From our parents and teachers, from relatives and strangers alike, we heard the admonition, "You can't do that! You are a Parsi!" uttered in a tone of incredulous horror. Moreover, being Zoroastrian meant feeling an urgent need to leave the world a better place than one found it. Even a child could and should do his bit to increase the store of good and defeat Ahriman in little ways. No gesture, however small, was meaningless. Henceforward every step we took barefoot would dry up the milk of a milch cow, and every time we blew out a candle it would dim the lustre of the firmament.

On the other hand every positive act would be added up to our account. And lest we forget, we were told the story of the tyrannical king who brought famine and torture to his land because of his greed and thirst for blood. He was also an avid hunter and owned a hunting hound of which he was very fond. One day when it was chained up, the thirsty animal was straining to get at a bowl of water just out of its reach. The tyrant kicked the bowl closer and the dog had its drink. When he died the king was claimed by Ahriman but his right foot went to Ahura Mazda for its single kind act.

So in order to help us build up our store of Good Deeds, we were made to volunteer for everything, whether we had any talent for it or no. Parsis took to Scouting like lemmings to the sea. The St. John's Ambulance Corps, the Slum Welfare Society, the City Beautification League, the Malaria Abatement Committee were all the brain children of old altruistic Parsis, and their manpower came from hundreds of reluctant little Parsi boys and girls. But to be fair, our parents volunteered as well. The only exception was the Fire Brigade. Till very recently no Parsi would throw water on the King of Kings and would rather stand by, even when it was his own house that was burning down.

It was equally important for us to be scrupulously honest. Once, when I was about seven, my mother beat and harangued me for an entire evening because she thought I was telling a lie. I had no way of escaping except by an admission which would then indeed be a lie. This insistence on an absolute moral standard has given Parsis an advantage in the market-place. Merchants and traders by profession, they compete with hundreds of other Indian castes doing the same thing. But their reputation for honesty and fair play gives them an edge over the rest. A Parsi's word is indeed his bond. I have seen Father bag large contracts for his factories even when his prices were higher than the other bids. He would explain this by saying that the purchaser knew he was dealing with a Parsi, and hence was sure that the entire consignment would match the original sample in quality.

Parsis like to think that Zoroastrianism is a scientific religion. Father avidly quoted a Parsi physicist who said that the ideas of atomic sub-particles, matter and anti-matter were all to be found clearly spelled out in our corpus. Even the gestures of the rituals had a scientific basis. The snapping of the sacred thread during prayer set up sound waves that cleared the area around the worshipper of negative ions. The use of charcoal in certain ceremonies was a filtration device and the use of metal objects instead of pottery had to do with the physical properties of materials. There was no room for superstitions in such a rational and natural system. But Hindu ideas of auspicious and inauspicious, of *karma* and *dharma* kept sneaking into our lives. Mother believed that peacocks and owls were unlucky. She invariably referred to Father's friend as "that owl". I thought she meant the woman was ugly, but the reference was to the owl as a harbinger of destruction and death. Father disparages my beautiful cat Mizzle as an insidious emissary of Ahriman. When Mother was exasperated beyond endurance with us she said we were enemies from her last life come to exact retribution in this one.

Mother had a horoscope, probably cast for her arranged marriage, although she refused to have any made for us. Hers was a long parchment scroll with a series of huge circles on it. She said it showed that her astrological temperament was "god-like," and that alone allowed her to withstand the horrors of being married to my father who was astrologically "devil-like." When we were young a South Indian Brahmin friend of Father's who was an accountant by profession and an astrologer by avocation had read that horoscope and predicted that she would die on her fifty-second birthday. And indeed his prophecy came true to the day! My sister said the night before she had smelled death so strongly, it woke her from her sleep. The next morning Mother was dead.

All her life Mother emphasized that superstition was merely a product of ignorance. There was no basis for belief in nonsense like black magic and omens. Still, one had to be careful. Although she would not put soot on her babies' temples to keep away the Evil Eye, she did insist that we not play outdoors during an eclipse. Once when we were driving to a hill-station we came to a crossroads outside a small village. Right in the middle of the intersection there was a little clay pot smothered in vermilion and flowers. We asked her what it was. "A superstitious ceremony by ignorant villagers to get rid of their sickness. They believe they have captured the disease in the pot, and it will enter the body of the person who carelessly steps over it." Then turning to Father she commanded him to drive into the ditch and around the pot.

One also had to be suitably wary of spiritually dangerous individuals like followers of Kali who kidnap children for human sacrifices or Aghoris who boil down people to the size of a pill in order to swallow their essence whole. Father had a close encounter with an Aghori when he went for an evening stroll around Kankaria Talao on his monthly trip to Ahmedabad. As he walked along the pleasant asphalt path around the lake he had an uneasy feeling of being followed, even though he heard no footsteps. Turning around he saw a barefoot, bare-chested man with matted hair and beggar's bowl quite a way behind him. But even at that distance there was no doubt it was an Aghori because his eyes glowed red like burning coals in the gathering dusk. Father quickened his pace but felt the man nearer, and the faster he walked the closer the Aghori seemed to get. Throwing dignity to the winds he sprinted the last few yards to the waiting car just an arm's length ahead of the Aghori. Whether such people had magical powers or not, it was best not to tangle with them.

Parsi pre-occupation with religion and identity makes conversion and mixed marriages the two greatest sins against the community. Father was vehemently intolerant of both. Very few Parsis were attracted to nineteenth-century mission Christianity. Maybe untouchables and tribals had something to gain from accepting Christ, but there was no obvious advantage in it for a prosperous and well-respected group like ours. Armed with the conviction that theirs was a rational, nay, even scientific belief system, they found it easy to resist the intellectual confusions of the Immaculate Conception and the Trinity.

Father reserved his most scathing attacks for Parsi women who went to church or visited the tombs of Muslim saints. Even his own mother and sister were not exempt from his ridicule when they attached themselves to a cult *guru* although this one happened to be a Zoroastrian himself. Father often told us the story of a certain Dadi Christ. He was a character who had been gang-pressed by missionaries into converting and used by them to address crowds in public on the glories of Christianity. Being a Parsi he quickly perceived the folly of his act but he had no way of backing out. So when he stood on his soap-box he would declare loudly in English, "Christ is my Saviour: He is the Lord!" and then add almost under his breath in the vernacular, "Don't believe me, not a word, I have been duped."

Once on our way to school Father observed a Parsi lady in traditional dress walking into the Cathedral at Mahim. He slowed the car down and shouted at her, "Why don't you go to a fire-temple, you fool?" The startled woman paused in her stride but recovered enough of her poise to shout back "Who the hell do you think you are? I'll do what I please!" adding an obscenity at the end. It made Father's day and we giggled the rest of the way to school as he re-enacted the scene over and over again, playing both roles.

Unlike conversion, the threat of the young marrying outsiders is very real and our elders put up a unified front against this unthinkable crime. At every turn we were reminded of our direct descent from that band of sailors who had charmed a recalcitrant potentate into giving us land and freedom of worship. We could not, must not, mix this heroic blood. It was our sacred duty to maintain its purity. We could not marry non-Parsis. But weren't we taught to be democratic and treat everyone as equals, I asked my Parsi school principal on a visit home? "We did not mean they are equal enough to marry," she answered crossly. And Father proclaimed loudly and often, "Intermarriage is the cause of the enfeeblement of the fiber of the community." "Genes will always show!" Mother declared, as if stating an indisputable scientific fact. Couldn't we see how different we were from the rest, how light in complexion and coloring? We weren't so sure. At school we had Marathi friends who had fair skin and green eyes. "Oh, that was because some of their ancestors married Portuguese adventurers on the south coast," Mother said, brushing aside our objection with only a slight distortion of history. So what about that lady with slanting eyes who dressed in men's pajama's and greeted us with a "Sahibji" in an unimpeachable Parsi accent? Father started to look glum. "Some of us were in the China trade and occasionally returned with more than trade goods," he explained ruefully. "She's just a house-keeper," said Mother with a knowing look, leaving us totally confused.

Then they would try a different tack. Didn't Parsis practically monopolize all the professions? A microscopic community in the midst of an ocean of other forms of humanity had provided ninety percent of the talent and brains for its adoptive country. Who was the best physician in Bombay? A Parsi. The brightest lawyer in the High Court? Again, a Parsi. Who conducted the Bombay Philharmonic? Who was the only man in India who could fix the great Mogul Emperor's English clock? The first Indian to be knighted by Our Majesty Queen Victoria? The first Indian woman to graduate from a university? Parsis, one and all. And did we notice that there were no Parsi beggars or thieves? Were we in our loathsome rebelliousness planning to dilute this distilled genetic genius?

Our experience of reality did not quite conform to this glorious portrait of the community. Most of the professionals we dealt with personally were not Parsis. The doctor we were taken to for exam fever was a Hindu in a *dhoti.* The math and science teachers in our Parsi school were Maharashtrians. The courtly looking business associate who visited Father and proffered us tiny mints out of an ornate silver box was a Banya. The Deputy Commissioner of Police who took me to the hospital after my accident was a Muslim, and the doctor who treated my eye disorder was a Khoja.

On the other hand, the Parsis we did meet and see were far from the mythic mold that Father was describing. We had observed a distinguished Parsi gentleman holding an animated conversation with a telegraph pole. We had seen Father give money to sad-looking unshaven men on the steps of the fire-temple even though they did not beg in the conventional way. Father's best friend was married to a horsey Englishwoman who encouraged the family retriever to consider them its Mummy and Daddy. The Parsi women we ran into at hill-stations verged on the bizarre. We met Lady L who wore special eyeglasses with little prongs to hold her droopy eyelids open wide so that she could check whether her sixty-year-old son was wearing his solar topee when he went for walks. And there was "Pavli" (a quarter-rupee), so called because she seemed to be in possession of a quarter of her faculties. She teetered on the gravelly slopes in high red heels and bright red lipstick singing in a falsetto, "Who has tasted a bee?"

Imperious old dowagers routinely threw priceless Venetian cut glass at their servants' heads and regularly left their large estates to their cockatoos. Mother knew two sisters, spinsters both, whose idea of being avant-garde involved cutting their hair in imitation of Veronica Lake and working for a firm producing birth control devices. The motley crowd of Parsis we met on Family Day at the Masonic Lodge seemed to confirm the average Indian's assessment of us as either corny or not quite *compos mentis.*

Even Father had to back off and admit that the men of the upper crust of the community were effete and the women eccentric. He attributed this to the twin upper-class customs of wet nursing and intermarriage. Father was flummoxed when faced with the behavior of a Parsi like Katey who married a doddering marquis for the sole reason of befriending the ghost resident in his Scottish castle. And the whole community despaired of Bapsy who came from a wealthy, titled family. Unmarried like most of the pampered and educated daughters of the well-to-do, she was the kind of flamboyant Parsi who gave us all a bad name. She was involved with all kinds of charities and her forte was arranging fashion shows and dinners. When a hired hand once pointed out to her that the head table at a party lacked a centerpiece, Bapsy climbed up and lay down, all two hundred pounds of herself, in the middle of the table with the query, "How's this for decoration?" She scandalized everyone even more by owning a race horse which she promptly baptized Zoroaster after the Prophet. It was a lacklustre animal that came in dead last at a chic race. The next day the Parsi newspapers erupted in censorious editorials and indignant letters to the press. One self appointed guardian of the Faith wrote in to proclaim, "To give a horse the Sacred Name of our Holy Prophet is sacrilegious, but to give it to a losing beast is pure perversion!" The whole incident generated so much hysteria that the community trustees appointed to look after the welfare of widows and orphans took it upon themselves to spend a fortune on a lawsuit to prevent a horse being called Zoroaster. They lost.

Wasn't this eccentricity among Parsis the result of in-breeding, we asked our parent? Thoroughly disgusted by our logic, Father would retreat into absolutes. "It can't be done. Crows and sparrows may sit on the same branch but they can't interbreed." Mother's answer was more matter-of-fact: "You won't inherit your great-grandfather's trust monies," was her short and simple reason for the taboo against marrying outsiders.

Closely linked to this xenophobia is the pre-occupation with keeping the Parsi way of life alive and uncontaminated. Language becomes the first and most potent weapon in that particular battle. Although he was forced to adopt an Indian language for sheer survival the Parsi has refused to learn it properly, even though he has been in India for as long as the Anglo-Saxons have been in England. Instead he speaks something called Parsi Gujarati which is met with hoots of laughter and malicious imitation by his true Gujarati neighbors. Yet it is an amazing tongue. It is rhythmic and ribald. It recapitulates the history of a people who in the interest of safety sought to be as close as possible to a whole succession of their rulers. It is an amalgam of Old Persian and Portuguese, Avestan and Gujarati, and now of course English. Those that study such things say that the uniqueness of each way of life is tied inextricably to the core vocabulary of its language. Parsis must be the exception that proves the rule. The most basic words in a Parsi's repertoire are borrowed: he calls upon his god in Avestan; the bread he eats is the Portuguese *pão*; the word for "language" he takes from Persian, as he does the word for "husband"; and for marriage he uses the Gujarati *lagan*. Thus a Parsi prays, eats and mates with foreign words. Perhaps that is the secret of his success as an immigrant. Like a chameleon's skin his words clothe him in the protective coloring of his interlocutor.

Parsi Gujarati is replete with obscene terms original and borrowed. Both men and women swear, but the vocabulary of abuse is different. Women tend to use the names of the lowest castes as oaths, whereas the men's terms have to do with bodily parts and functions. Although we were surrounded by these sounds everywhere, we were not supposed to understand them and certainly not allowed to use them ourselves. But lapses did occur occasionally. One summer I suffered a sudden outbreak of large boils all over my body. Father swore as he inspected me. A few hours later the old neighbor upstairs clucked in sympathy over my pitiful appearance. "Oh, don't worry," I airily reassured her, "the mother fuckers will go away in a week." The shocked woman ran down to alert Mother to my linguistic precocity.

The Parsi patois is not a literary language. When he wants to put pen to paper a Parsi has to shift into sanskritized Gujarati or Oxford

English. But his is a mimic's tongue full of onomatopoeic words recreating nature exactly in human accents. It has a word that lets me describe the sound of animal paws on dry leaves or that of slippered feet on wooden floors. In one achingly precise word I can convey the sight of softly falling rain that has not yet developed full-blown drops. I can sum up in one deprecating adjective the self-conscious coyness of a little girl showing off in her party dress. But it does not let me express irony or cold calculating hate. For that I need English. I dream and feel in my mother-tongue but I reflect, reason and devastate in English. I learned its limitless potential by devouring the Victorian novels in the school library. There is nothing to match, in any language that I know, the bilious invective of a Thackeray, the lachrymose bathos of a Dickens, or the muscular cadence of a Thomas Hardy. Between the ages of eleven and sixteen I read at least three tomes a week, even though it meant enduring Mother's accusing plaint, "Are you again into that mush?" and finishing the book by flashlight under a suffocating blanket. I would have read more if it were not for the meagerness of the supply and Mother's attitude that books were merely a clever way of shirking housework. This is inexplicable given the fact that she was the first to grab the magazines including the children's weekly, and carefully smoothed out and read the bits of newsprint wrapped around the daily shopping.

The Englishness of our speech has its counterpart in the home. A Parsi house invariably exudes a faintly foreign air of Chippendale and chintz. It is totally unlike a Hindu home with its mattresses on the floor and pictures of cross-eyed goddesses sticking out their blood-stained tongues. No Parsi residence is complete without a cupboard full of Wedgwood, its reproduction of Gainsborough's "Blue Boy", and a lithograph of Queen Victoria at her least amused. No member of the Royal Family is ever referred to by a Parsi without the qualifying possessive "our", as in "our Prince Philip". A piano usually stands four square in the living room, carefully draped in Chinese jacquard silk. His Master's Voice sits in the opposite corner with a stack of music hall records.

The foreign influence on a Parsi home stops at the kitchen door. Aside from Chivers' marmalade and Black Magic chocolates, Parsi food is an Indianized version of Persian cuisine with a Goanese flourish added by the cook. And it is eaten with the fingers, the imported silverware being reserved for guests or special occasions.

Our home was free of any such pro-British sentiments, Mother being stoutly anti-imperialist. In the hot and heady days of the Quit India Movement she had followed the Mahatma and worn homespun *khadi*, although right after Independence she reverted to French chiffons and English cambric. The most she would permit was a photograph of the Venus de Milo and crockery with the Tower of London painted on it. However, she had nothing but admiration for English arts and letters. She quoted the Romantic poets with great feeling. We were encouraged to debate the merits of Utilitarianism and Sufism with equal zeal without regard to their origin. "The greatest good of the greatest number" became a Parsi idea in my father's hands and "No man is an island entire unto himself" the family creed. In case we got an inflated idea of our say in our destiny, we also heard "Though the mills of God grind slowly, yet they grind exceeding small." And all this to the strains of Bach or John Philip Sousa! This omnivorous inclusiveness of the Parsi ethos has stood us in good stead as we have sought to make our lives among strangers abroad. Neither headlong flight from our past nor an ardent embracing of our present has enabled us to shed even one jot of our Parsiness.

EIGHT

He who teaches is a giver of eyes
— Sanskrit proverb

One of the unadulterated pleasures of my childhood was going to school. I started at three at a nursery or pre-school run by two Parsi sisters in their home. Since it was four houses away but within the fenced compound I walked there by myself armed with slate and pencil. We were taught the Gujarati and English alphabets, numbers, and nursery rhymes in both languages. They also drilled us in English word lists like the names of colors and parts of the body. Beyond that our comprehension of English was nil. We merely imitated and memorized the sound, but that did not prevent us from making inspired guesses at the meanings. As we sang out "Tiggy tiggy touchwood, my black hen. . ." we stuck out and waved our little hands energetically. This left me puzzled, since mine were distinctly a pinkish beige and not black at all. This habit of intuiting meanings has persisted. Later when I read *The Hunchback of Notre Dame* without benefit of Latin I wondered why Quasimodo had a Japanese name and how he was connected to the famed house of Mikimoto whose ads for pearl jewelry Mother so admired.

At four I transferred to a real school. It was a private Parsi infants' and girls' school where Mother had taught for a while. It had been endowed by two public-spirited men interested in female education. Its current benefactress was Lady Jehangir. She belonged to the famed Readymoney family whose ancestor had been knighted after bailing out the East India Company with a few cartloads of silver coins during the Maratha Wars. She was an erect old lady with bluish-white hair who always wore a different diamond brooch on her shoulder when she attended the annual prize-giving ceremony. Mother chose this school for us because the standard of education in the government-run schools was too low, while the Catholic schools according to Mother turned out girls who were arrogant and ignorant of their own language and cultural heritage. It was she who took me there the first day. "She's quite ready for Second Standard", she declared to the principal. "How old is she?" asked Miss Bana, looking me over. "Four, almost."

"She goes to kindergarten," said Miss Bana with her severest frown. Immediately Mother put on her most combative expression. She whipped out a book from her bag and thrust it under my nose. "Read!" she commanded. Miss Bana was watching me with pursed lips. I did not like being put on trial so I stared at the page. Mother gave me a little shove, "Go on! you could do it well enough yesterday." It was a poem about a cat. I stared fixedly at the page until the black letters burst their edges and the cat's whiskers started to wriggle. "She's playing stupid," said Mother exasperatedly. "I want to speak to you alone," declared Miss Bana. The principal won that round, and I walked over to the Infants' School to a classroom full of singing children and rocking horses. Mother was so angry she stormed home without telling me she was leaving. I watched the classroom door all day for her. That evening she complained to Father about my disgraceful defiance. He gave me an approving look for this first act of independent thinking on my part, and thenceforth it was he who took a child to be admitted to school.

Once I got used to the presence of the other children, school was heaven. It remained for me an oasis of orderly calm routine for twelve happy years with only that brief, miserable interlude at the boarding school. The school was in a Parsi residential area at Dadar. It had a couple of two-storey buildings. When you finished Fourth Standard you got to walk ceremonially from the little school to the big one. On each floor of the Primary School building a row of classrooms was flanked by corridors. In one there were tables and benches where we ate lunch. The other was used for playing jacks during recess as well as for prayers every morning and evening. We sang "Abide with Me" and "Lead, Kindly Light," Gandhi's favorite hymn, or recited Zoroastrian prayers or Hindu *bhajans*. At the end of this building was a sandpit surrounded by a two-foot high wall. I would hide flat on my stomach close to it and read novels when I was supposed to be playing hockey with the class on the nearby field. The kindergartners didn't seem to mind my presence at all.

The big school had huge windows through which the hot breezes blew all day. We could look out and see the dancing leaves of the neem trees, and the owl outside the geography room watched us unblinkingly as we rattled off the names of the capital cities of Europe. The big bell hanging outside marked the end of every period. Sometimes the peon would forget, and a child would be sent to "go tell the *hamal* to ring the bell!" The atmosphere inside was one of overwhelming peacefulness, in spite of the sound of chanting children or an occasional sob from a miscreant made to stand in the corridor for its sins.

Between the buildings lay lawns and flower gardens. The botany teacher maintained these with the help of a toothless *mali* who smiled and nodded at instructions and then did exactly what he thought fit. During her class we would stand around the flower beds taking petunias apart with hairpins as she rhapsodized over the symmetry of the seed-box. There was a third structure which looked like a cross between a barn and a greenhouse. This was the play-shed with flake-board on the floor, gym bars along the walls, and a stage at one end. It was used for P.T. classes and Monday-morning school assemblies. Miss Banaji pounded out Schubert's *Marche Militaire* on the black baby grand as each class filed in arranged according to height. I was usually at the head of my class.

We also gathered in the playshed for lectures by guests whom we listened to sitting cross-legged on the floor. Once an English missionary gave a talk about the rules of etiquette which included never opening an umbrella indoors and, inexplicably, the proper way of handling salt cellars, an item never present on an Indian dining table. There was another high-pitched Parsi lady who was a regular. She was pious, always dressed in white, and covered her head demurely with the end of her sari. She droned on about the Seven Heavenly Planes for years till we had had enough. During one of her monthly talks the principal and vice-principal were absent. As she began five hundred little girls started whispering and giggling. The murmur grew into a steady hum. The teachers glared. Still the noise continued to grow louder till one of the senior teachers said, "No talking!" with an apologetic nod to the speaker. The noise seemed to ebb but within minutes swelled once again to a semi-roar. The speaker stopped talking, hoping to shame her audience into silence. Girls sitting closest to the teachers were being scolded. A semblance of order was restored. The guest took a deep breath and began, "The progression from the Fourth to the Fifth Level is beset by obstacles. . ." Suddenly as if possessed the five hundred started clapping and stamping their feet. The power of the mob was awesome to behold. The speaker fled, the teachers were in a state of shock; never in the history of the school had such an act of mutiny occurred. The whole school was made to stand in class for the rest of the day but the woman was struck off the list of guest speakers and was never seen again.

Our favorite was a twinkly-eyed, pink-cheeked Zoroastrian priest who acted out stories from the *Shah Nameh.*

Of course class plays, poetry recitations, elocution competitions and such other events were also held on the large stage in the playshed.

The actors had to climb onto the stage via the garden. Our teachers preferred plays that called for a large cast so that no child would be without a role. If not, they improvised by sending a footman as well as the butler to announce Lady Bracknell's arrival, or created crowds of housemaids and extraneous Greek choruses that wilted in the wings. We were good; we won several city-wide drama competitions. Occasionally students were allowed to write their own material. I wrote several household comedies in Hindi, with the inevitable bumbling servant who had all the laugh-lines.

Our school was one of five in the city designated an Experimental School. But this did not mean a deviation from the set curriculum or the prescribed textbooks since we still had to be prepared for the S.S.C. examination. However, the teachers could think up extra-curricular activities to develop our moral character and leadership qualities. So we had things like teacher-for-a-day, when older girls dressed up like teachers and took all the classes. The principal-for-the-day once took advantage of her office to declare a holiday. On hearing of it the real principal charged out of the common-room to exercise her veto power.

Each class had an appointed monitor who maintained discipline between classes and during recesses. It says something about our habit of obedience that we listened to our monitors with as much deference as to teachers. The monitor of the Eleventh Standard was also the head-girl. In the year when it was the turn of someone in my class, the civics teacher decided it would be good training in citizenship to have the school elect a head-girl. Each class got weeks of lectures on the political and moral advantages of self-government, and one's obligation to be worthy of this privilege. We were drilled in the correct procedures of balloting and told about the duties of election judges. A slate of candidates went around tacking posters with their symbols to everything in sight, including the stakes that held up the pea plants in the garden. In India each political candidate must have a graphic visual symbol so that the illiterate masses can identify him. Although we could read, the teachers pedantically insisted our election had to be exactly like the real thing. So we came up with slogans and symbols which were to say the least original. "Bug out with Bapsy!" said one, with a large spider on it; "A rose is a rose is a Rita" said another, with a dead pink rose glued to it. The experiment in self-rule degenerated into mob hysteria as rumors of intimidation and pay-offs circulated in the corridors. On election day, as the official press, I made up stories of ballot-stuffing and fraud in imitation of the best *Blitz* reportorial style. The Poodle won. The teachers judged us not ready for democracy and reinstated head-girlship by appointment.

Each year in March we went to a class picnic. The usual spot was Aarey Dairy, a model automated milk pasteurization plant which was opened in the 1950s as part of India's first Five Year Plan. Set in several hundred acres of parkland on the outskirts of the city, it soon became a mecca for busloads of schoolchildren. Sometimes we were taken to Pavai or Vihar Lake, the huge reservoirs that supplied the city with its drinking water. We had to wear hats with our uniforms on picnics. Most of the girls wore straw ones with large brims or beribboned boaters. My parents' idea of a hat for a little girl was a small khaki solar *topee* complete with leather chinstrap. Each child brought her own lunch, but the food was shared. It was nice to eat the other girls' spice-laden food as a change from Mother's healthy bland stuff. Occasionally we were taken to the films. The first one I ever saw was Walt Disney's "The Living Desert". I was fifteen. The whole Secondary School went and two hundred girls sucked in their breath audibly as spines on cacti splashed open into dazzling flowers. The close-up of centipedes met similarly with a united gasp of revulsion. It was always painful stepping out in the tropical sun at the end of the film. "Alexander the Great" was a disaster because we all fell asleep from the boredom of watching endless cavalry charges and the unaccustomed cold of the air-conditioned theater.

One of the nicest things about school was that I could read without

Mother's constant interruptions. I read during the recesses and between classes. I read as I walked to the cooking or embroidery class or the gym. I hid and read during games. I even read during classes. It was possible to do this by keeping the textbook on the top of the desk and a novel open on my lap. If I sat far enough back on the bench I could see both books without really having to move my head. Of course I never had any problem following a lecture while I was reading, so no teacher was ever able to ambush me with a question I failed to hear. I considered myself quite clever for getting away with this for seven years. It is clear to me now that the teachers were perfectly aware of what I was doing. But they had enough insight into my personality and enough confidence in my abilities to leave me to it. I read anything I could get hold of with equal passion.

The school library provided the classics: Eliot, Alcott, Austin, as well as Enid Blyton. The thrills came from adventure stories begged from classmates who belonged to a penny lending library. It circulated the School Girl Books, a series published in London but in a pirated edition. They were printed on miserable, almost brown paper, four columns to a page, in a type so small it left one invariably with a severe headache. And when I couldn't beg, borrow or steal a read I simply turned back to the first page of the book I had just finished.

All this reading left me no time or inclination for close friendships with other girls. I got along with them all right but I was never part of any clique, nor did I have a best friend for a very long time. Most of the girls did not particularly like me and it did not matter to me that they didn't since the teachers did. It was not that I was shy or snobbish; I just did not have any confidences to exchange with them. But all this changed when a new girl joined my class in the Seventh Standard. She was an upper-caste Punjabi and I still do not know which school she came from. I liked her immediately. She had shy eyes, a reserved manner, and the most serene expression I had ever seen. Although she was short and plump her face was beautiful in a very different way from the Parsi girls. She had a long straight nose whose strength was softened by a perfect bow mouth that turned up at the corners. She saw me looking at her on the first day of school and gave me a smile that transformed her face. I was fascinated by her self-possession. She became my first and only real friend and the first person outside the family that I learned to love. For the next five years of High School and two of College we sat next to each other in class. In all those years we did not have a single difference of opinion. She was brilliant and shared my fascination with words. She got better marks than I at Hindi, French and sometimes algebra but I didn't mind in the least. I loved to make her smile.

She lived within walking distance of school and invited me to go home with her for lunch one day. I knew my parents would not approve but I accepted anyway. And from that day on her mother and sister-in-law treated me like a daughter of the family. I had lunch at her home every school day for years without ever telling my parents. Her mother would serve both of us on the same *thali.* I was too ignorant of caste rules then to appreciate this gesture of unreserved acceptance extended to me. And I was clumsy at sitting on the floor and eating with my hands. My friend complained when I used both hands to tear the bread or sniffed the aroma of dishes new to me before tasting them. We never saw each other outside school hours, since we both came from homes where the parents strictly controlled our free time.

I admired my friend for what I could not be myself. She radiated a patient calm which contrasted sharply with my anxious, frantic intensity. I knew she would become the kind of woman I wished I could be, the kind who can silence barking dogs and still crying children by merely appearing in their presence. In the third year of College she left to specialize in psychology at St. Xavier's, while I stuck it out with Henry the Eighth at Elphinstone. But we saw each other as frequently as we could. A few months before the baccalaureate exam her parents arranged her marriage. When I objected vehemently to her mother she said softly, "You can't live in the river and be enemies with the crocodile; society says a woman is first and foremost a wife and mother. This is a good and respectable family we have found for her." I tried to make her run away from home but she was a more dutiful daughter than I, and since then I have lost her. She has haunted my dreams for over a decade now. One day soon I will have to go in search of her.

Most of our schoolteachers were single Parsi women who had chosen this profession knowing that it meant sacrificing marriage and motherhood. They were exceptional people who would have succeeded at any career. Above all they were gifted teachers.

There was Roshan Auntie, school incarnate for thirty lucky kindergartners each year for over five decades. I was one of them. She taught us to read by reading aloud for hours each day. She taught us to write by writing "cat" and "bat" on the first line of each of our copy books which we then painfully tried to imitate on the next five lines. I never heard her criticize any of our clumsy attempts. She would hold a pudgy little fist desperately clutching a pencil, and say mildly, "Don't you think a "c" looks better with a round tummy?" She could sing *Baa-Baa Black Sheep* for the millionth time with all the delight of having just invented it for our express benefit. We believed her totally when she said that one's lies showed in one's eyes, and that when pets and children died they went to a very special flower garden. Miss Mehta's love of geography was so contagious we decided to visit every place ever mentioned in the *National Geographic*. She was absolutely impartial and we knew when we had disappointed her without her uttering a word of reproach. In Mrs. Shroff's literature class a Chesterton essay became a debate about private values and public ethics. So impressive were these women that on weekends all we could think of doing was putting on one of Mother's *saris* and playing our teachers.

There were no male teachers employed, but as time went on there seemed to be a shortage of teachers of certain subjects. So very reluctantly the principal engaged two men. The first was a temporary who replaced the math teacher. He was a very young Goanese who dressed in tight pants, leather ties, and slicked back his hair with tons of coconut oil. He had the habit of exclaiming, "What man!" when exasperated, which sounded very avant-garde to our ears. Large crowds of spaniel-eyed girls followed him up and down the corridors and hung about the teachers' common-room hoping to catch a glimpse of the idol. The other male teacher was the Hindi master. He was gruff and played favorites. Not being handsome in the film-star mould he had a limited number of devotees. We gave him a very hard time because we knew that he could not possibly go to complain to the female principal that he was unable to control a bunch of girls.

Our teachers felt passionately about knowledge and about us. They wanted to form us into thinking women who would make enlightened mothers and teachers. They nurtured our minds but thought it infinitely more important to nurture our characters. It seemed perfectly natural to us that a discussion of Robert Burns should end up as a lecture on moral philosophy. I can hear my English teacher's voice instructing, "When you want something, first ask yourself, "Do I deserve it?" If you can honestly answer "Yes", then don't let anything stand in the way of achieving it." Their credo was "An educated woman can do anything." And so we had to be good at science as well as cooking. Looking at my sorry piece of handiwork my crafts teacher remarked caustically, "Do not think that because you are clever you can be unwomanly!" The greatest stress was on the cultivation of compassion and empathy. If you finished the algebra exercises in half the allotted time you had to help the failing student with hers. If you forgot to cover your books you were made to stand bare-headed in the sun "to feel what the book must be feeling without its clothes." It is only now as a teacher myself that I realize how very remarkable these women were in their capacity to nurture and inspire an entire generation.

NINE

What dire offence from amorous causes springs,
What mighty contests rise from trivial things.
— Alexander Pope

When they were first married Father took Mother to the site of a huge unfinished circular house facing the ocean at Bandra. As they walked through the roofless rooms hand-in-hand, he said something that startled her. "We shall have enough children to fill every room in a house as big as this!" She wasn't thrilled, but kept her peace for the moment. Many years later she related this to me as an illustration of his eccentricity. I think however that the need to nurture is my father's most genuine and deep-seated impulse. And it extends to all children. True, he prefers the child to be either pretty or precocious, but any child at all can lay claim to his sympathy and attention. He knew all my classmates even though he saw them only for a few minutes as they trooped in and out of school each day. He always had a word of praise for one or a teasing remark for another. It made him happy to watch them going to school. He said they put him in mind of little angels in their white uniforms.

Where our welfare was concerned Father's anxiety was unlimited and extended into the realm of the metaphysical. Among Parsis, the birth of a child calls for several rituals which are to be performed by the elder females of the family. The absence of any such person in our home did not deter Father from coercing the Fates in our favor. He prepared for Mother's arrival home with a new baby with great respect for the details. He would clean the floor outside the entrance way and decorate it better than any woman. He made a design in powdered chalk which had a central pinwheel of seven auspicious fish motifs. He linked this to the corners with floral crescents. The design would have the prescribed odd number of elements and was perfectly centered and proportioned. He hung a thick fragrant garland on the doorway itself. Before Mother crossed the threshold he circled her head seven times each with a coconut, a trayful of water, and an egg. Then Mother and Baby would have red vermilion applied to their foreheads and the tops of their feet.

Late on the evening of the sixth day after birth Father prepared for the arrival of the angel who would write the child's future. Since Mother was still in an impure state it was he who set up the tray with offerings of rice, coconut, rosewater and silver coins on the round glass tea-table. Next to the tray he put down a crisp sheet of foolscap with the baby's name inscribed at the top together with an old-fashioned pen and inkwell for the angel to transact its business. After lighting a lamp Father retired to another room where he sat up praying for the rest of the night in order to inspire the heavenly guest to be generous. At sunrise the next day he carefully and reverentially filed away the sheet of paper with the previous ones in his cupboard.

I have always felt a special quality in my Father's love for me. He was known as *my* father by the entire school including the teachers, which infuriated my sisters no end. It was he who picked my name, a strong one full of harsh consonants. Mother resisted as long as she could but you can't call a little girl Bright-eyes for ever! So finally he had his way and now I have a totally unpronounceable name. He was fond of telling me how being his first child I had to put up with his inexperience. In their poverty my parents could not afford a crib, not even a wicker basket, for their first newborn. Father absolutely refused to let Mother take me to bed with them because he had heard of a case where a woman turning in her sleep had smothered her infant. So for the first four months of my life I stayed on the seat of an easy-chair. This was not too happy a solution since the seat sloped backwards and I kept sliding and hitting my head on the cane back. Whenever I moved my limbs I bruised them on its wooden arms, till Father laboriously wrapped each bit of exposed wood with one of Mother's soft *saris.* Once I was old enough to sit up he devised amusements for me. He would tear up a sheet of *The Times* into twelve squares and watch and help as I stacked them on my head. His favorite game was to hold me up to the sun and whip me quickly into the shadow to watch my pupils dilate.

And to his great delight I started to talk very early. I had impressed everyone on that first Independence Day as I rode in the tram with him watching the illuminated city. Thrilled by millions of lights, the noise and the crowds, I kept up a running commentary of exclamations till an old woman marvelled at how tiny I was for my age. "She's only eleven months," said Father proudly. "Oh no, you must never say that," the woman shot back, "you must protect her from envious strangers; tell them she's two-and-a-half but stunted!"

Father was also amazed by my capacity to amuse myself. According to him I could spend hours in absolute concentration with whatever was at hand. And I never cried, with one exception. Punctually as an alarm going off I would scream one minute past feeding time. The first time this happened when he was alone with me my ferocious yelling so unnerved him that he dropped the bottle. After that he always had everything prepared in advance and managed to cut me off in mid-wail with a quick thrust of the nipple. He found my equanimity a great contrast to my brother. He was utterly thrilled when he received the news at work that he had had a son. He rushed home to pick me up before going to the hospital. He was so excited, he said, that he did not even notice that I had lost one brand-new shoe on the way. "I walked back slowly over the whole route twice looking for your little white shoe," he was reminiscing once. "Red!" snapped Mother, "no wonder you didn't find it!"

My verbal precocity encouraged Mother to chat with me as she went about her work. Once returning home unexpectedly in the middle of the day, Father heard her conversing cheerfully and suspected she had a lover. He carefully climbed over the balcony, only to find her in a serious discussion with me. She also taught me nursery rhymes and folk tales. As soon as I had a few stories and songs under my belt I took to entertaining the neighbors. I became a great favorite with the teenage children of the widow next door and they carried me off at every opportunity. Soon their large circle of school-friends collected me regularly for their evening conclaves. The girls endlessly combed and braided my long hair and the boys swung me around by my arms. I had my favorites amongst them. There was Dara, quiet and broad-shouldered, who made sure I wasn't handled too roughly. I liked Noshir who tickled my nose with the tip of a crow's feather.

My best performance I reserved for Father. Watching him rub his weary eyes I would inquire about the exact nature of the pain. To his amusement I got the words garbled. So he would let me repeat my question several times before accepting the medicine I made up in the corner and letting me cast a get-well spell on him. Mother never let me worry about her or take care of her.

I have always needed to look after something. One day a little dog followed me home from my evening excursion with the neighbors. Mother would not let him in so I talked to him through the door for several hours. At dinner I insisted on sharing my food. For the next few days I was extremely contented with my new-found friend who listened patiently to my songs. Then he suddenly disappeared. I worried and wept and my parents were miserable at my unhappiness. Several weeks later I was playing inside the house when I heard a low soft yelp at the door. My dog had come back! I got Mother to let me out. There he stood looking at me, slowly wagging his tail. I brought him some bread and milk and then some chocolate. He didn't even glance at the food but just kept staring at me. Suddenly he lay down and stopped moving altogether. Mother quickly dragged me inside and consolingly said that he had gone to sleep and that I wasn't to disturb him for the rest of the day. Next day she told me he had merely come to thank me for my past kindness and returned to his owner. That year for my third birthday Father had an artist friend paint me a card. It had a collie done in oils and was inscribed in my father's beautiful hand. For years the card lay in Mother's biscuit tin full of sentimental odds and ends. I wish I had retrieved it before I left home.

My parents were proud of the fact that I accepted responsibility willingly. They made no bones about the fact that I was in charge in their absence and the younger children as well as the servants were under my supervision. This began when Mother went to the hospital to have a baby: I was only four. On one such occasion the servant-girl used the opportunity to take a wad of banknotes from the cupboard and secreted them in her clothes. She did not know I was watching quietly from the other room. When my parents got back I promptly reported the theft in great detail. Without further ado Mother yanked the women's *sari* off at the waist. Out fell the bundle of crisp new notes. After dispensing with the wailing, half-dressed woman Mother praised my uncanny powers of observation. Father applauded my uncommon presence of mind in not confronting the servant myself and giving the game away. For a few days I was the child wonder who had foiled a criminal. "So young and she caught a thief!" the neighbors would exclaim in awe as I came into view.

Father liked to see his family look like a family. He liked us in matching clothes. Mother always bought half a bolt of cloth, enough to make a house-coat for herself and a smock for the newest baby. That way, said Father, everyone could see the baby had emerged from the mother. He was also fond of taking family photographs. This was an elaborate procedure. We all had to be brushed and polished. Next, he had to pose us properly in the light. Then the camera was set up on a tripod with delayed exposure. As soon as he had pressed the button he would make a wild dash to get behind the group. He always had a slightly vexed expression in these family photographs.

Did he think of his children as an undifferentiated whole? Unconstrained by Freud, Indian parents encourage their children to take sides between them. "Whose child are you, Mummy's or Daddy's?" they ask, and mine were no exception. My younger sister as a baby solved the problem two-handedly by pointing to both of them simultaneously. In our turn we anxiously looked for signs that a parent did not love a sibling more than ourselves. I had no idea how much it irked my brother that Father chose me to sit up with him late in the night to listen to his collection of classical records. "The Secret World of father and daughter," my brother calls it in his writing. And to me it seemed that Mother always took his side when he fought with one of us.

For Father that question was answered most dramatically at the time of my accident. When I was in high school my sisters and I were being chauffeured home. Mother had asked me to run an errand for her. In my haste I dashed across a street and got knocked down by a double-decker bus. Luckily it was inching its way forward in the traffic and I happened to fall neatly in between the front wheels. I was pulled out by the crowd fully conscious and intact except for a profusely bleeding chin. An off-duty police inspector happened upon the scene and decided to take me to a hospital. I however sat on the curb insisting I would not budge until my father was summoned. So he made a deal with me: If I went right away to the hospital he would personally phone my father and ask him to meet us there.

Off I went to get my chin stitched while the inspector phoned Father at the mills. He said "Your daughter was involved in an accident. She's perfectly all right except for a bump or two. Please collect her at the hospital." But he had left out the crucial bit of information about which daughter was involved, and Father started to imagine which one. That was when he realized he had no favorites among his children. He wanted to will it to have been a particular child but could not do so. "It can't be the eldest because she is physically the weakest and won't survive", he argued with himself. "I can't bear to lose my loyal middle one; the smallest is too young to die yet." He realized he could not choose which one it would hurt him the least to lose. When he walked into the emergency room the only thing he said was "How could you?" and all my composure fled instantly. I broke into sobs from relief at his presence. He decided to take me immediately for observation and tests to the Parsi General Hospital. There I was examined by a neurologist who was a retired colonel. He had a glass eye, a fierce moustache and parade-ground posture. My pulse elevated from sheer fright as he looked me over with his one good eye. For the next week in the hospital I had Father to myself day and night. Till I returned my schoolmates were made to say an extra prayer every day at assembly for my recovery.

Mother tended not to make distinctions between us and treated us with equal severity. She preferred babies to children anyway and so the newest arrival got all her attention. She was never more beautiful than when she was pregnant nor more calm than when she was nursing. She had miscarried a child just before me in the sixth month. It must have grieved her deeply because she talked of that one to us. "That baby had your father's nose and perfect little fingernails. At the hospital they threw her on the floor. I wanted to pick her up and at least wrap her in a white cloth but I was too weak to move. The sweeper woman took her away saying, "It's just garbage!"

She fell asleep crying and had a dream. A bright and shiny woman dressed in blue asked her not to mourn. "I promise you I will give you many more children," the lady said. A year later during the Feast of Mount Mary I was born. Legend says that a fisherman had caught a statue of the Virgin in his net and was bidden in a dream to erect a church for her. Thus the Shrine of Our Lady of the Mount was built on the hill next to the ocean at Bandra. Every September a week-long fair is held to commemorate the Vision. On a whim on my first birthday Mother asked to be taken to the fair. It was only when she filed past the gold-bedecked statue of the Virgin with the other pilgrims that she realized this was the lady of her dream. She had indeed kept her promise.

There is no doubt that Father worried about his daughters' futures. He could think and plan for our marriages without facing the fact that it would involve our getting to know flesh-and-blood males. While I was still very young he took me to his bank in order to "reassure you of your future," as he put it. He wouldn't utter a word more but looked very mysterious and excited. We walked through a marble and mahogany lobby to a polished brass elevator. We descended in it slowly to the bowels of the building. We were now in the safety deposit area reserved for special customers. Father signed a leather-covered ledger and uttered the password to a worried looking clerk. As soon as he was handed his grey steel box Father and I went into a strange opaque glass cage. Then he ordered me to close my eyes and hold out my hands. Suddenly I felt a great weight and almost dropped it. Opening my eyes I found a bright gold brick in my extended palms. Solemnly Father explained, "When you girls grow up I will personally saw this into three equal parts for your dowries." And then he added, "Never give or sign over anything you get from me to your husband." In later years he did not let any man even approach a daughter of his and the gold brick was recently donated to charity.

Their own unorthodox marriage and disreputable divorce had cut my parents off from other Parsi families who might have provided potential spouses for us. They avoided the onerous duty of arranging our marriages by refusing to face the fact that we were grown up. At the same time they adamantly refused to allow us the freedom to choose our own partners on the peculiar ground that their choice had turned out to be a disaster. Mother's experience of her earlier arranged marriage was even worse. She told us garbled tales of an infatuated suitor trying to kidnap her whilst her father and aunt tried to make her consent to one of a string of proposals that kept pouring in from as far away as Karachi and Durban. But she kept hoping for one from her cousin, the calm quiet one who engaged her in friendly banter as she sat spinning the sacred thread on the veranda of her father's house in Navsari. His mother however had set her heart on a wealthy daughter-in-law and so he walked away from his poor cousin. I know in later years he phoned her occasionally. She would shoo us away as she talked in cryptic half sentences. The rest of the day she appeared preoccupied. Young as I was, I remember wondering whether my mother might not have been a more contented woman if she had somehow been closer to this mysterious stranger on the telephone. Finally, giving way to the threats and entreaties of her relatives, she decided to say yes to the very next proposal that came in. It happened to be from a mild but mediocre bank accountant from Bombay who lived in an extended family of over fifty souls. She was all of seventeen. "He never mistreated me like your father," was all she would tell us about him. But she admitted that she did not love him and could not bear the intellectual boredom of being married to him. Even her insane mother whom she dutifully visited with her new husband commented "Not bright enough for you, my dear!" Mother hated his possessive sisters and relatives. "Villagers with petty minds and small preoccupations," she said of them, and her greatest regret was that her own daughter by that marriage grew up to be like those women.

When she left that household she walked out with only the clothes she had brought from her father's house. She was forced to leave her six-year-old daughter behind. Her husband seemed to harbor no resentment at her defection nor anger against my father who had taken her away from him. He never remarried and worried about her physical and spiritual well-being for the rest of her life. The winter she left him was an unusually cold one. He waited with her brown fur coat at Apollo Bunder where he knew she habitually went for evening walks. I do not think she wore the coat even once and we used it as a tent or a royal cape in our play. After some years he came to our house to visit her or more correctly to look at her, since much of the time was passed in silence. When leaving he would always tell her precisely what prayers he would be reciting and rituals he would be performing to counteract the particular configuration of planets currently affecting her horoscope. Mother seemed to be unmoved by these encounters with him.

The man's relatives were not quite so generous with Mother. They retaliated by refusing to allow her to see her daughter. She tried to circumvent their dictate by going to the child's school. When they heard of it they locked the little girl in a room without food for three days. The next time Mother appeared at the school-yard she ran away. It was ten years later when she was about to be married herself that she consented to see Mother again. Her aunts had arranged that she should marry her cousin who was raised in the same household with her and for whom she had felt a secret childhood infatuation.

A meeting was set up one evening at Bandra beach. We sat tensely with Father in the car as Mother walked out alone. In the distance a slim young girl in a flowered dress sat like a mermaid on a big black rock, her long hair golden in the light of the setting sun. As Mother approached her she did something quite astounding to us. She started to bow at Mother's feet. We reserved that formal gesture for the fire-temple and corpses passing in the street. Mother stepped back quickly and caught her in an embrace. In less than ten minutes she was back dabbing her eyes. She did not attend her daughter's wedding. A month later when the girl finally came to our house to show Mother her new husband we knew she was our sister. She looked exactly like Mother with her high brow and liquid brown eyes in spite of her peculiar gestures and old women's talk.

Given her own awful experience with the institution of the arranged marriage, it was no surprise that Mother firmly refused to negotiate any such deal for us. When her own sister suggested a possible match between her eldest son and me Mother dismissed the idea outright on the grounds that each person had to make his own destiny. However she panicked when I showed signs of defecting permanently to America. So when I returned home for a short holiday she dredged up a relative who in turn dug up a potential husband for me. On a mid-afternoon in May, when the heat had silenced even the crows, the relative turned up at the house accompanied by a thin wispy man dressed in a three-piece wool suit. Mother was drowsing. I had just emerged from the bath, and the house was in disarray. Cross at being disturbed at that odd hour I answered the door with my head wrapped in a towel and a scowl on my face. I showed the guests to the living room and went to awaken Mother. "Something is fishy!" said my ever-suspicious sister darkly. Mother acted flustered when I informed her of the visitors. She started to give me a stream of orders: "For God's sake, brush your hair! And why are you wearing that dress? Go make some tea and bring it in yourself; no, come and talk to our guests first." "What about?" I asked stupidly, as my sister glared at the stranger through a shutter. The relative made conversation as the young man sat wordless on the edge of the sofa. Suddenly turning to me the older man asked, "When will you return permanently from the U.S.?" "Oh, maybe in ten years to show my children where I grew up," I replied off-handedly. The stranger winced visibly and retreated further into a corner of the sofa. After half an hour they left. I was still puzzled by the whole thing but my sister kept muttering "It's a plot!"

That evening after her customary prayers Mother summoned me to her side. "So what shall I say?" she asked. I stood uncomprehending. She burst out, "Don't be daft! Did you or did you not like the young man?" Then it dawned on me that my Mother had betrayed me. She had sneaked in a suitor without even talking to me about it. "That mouse? That nitwit who did not have enough sense not to wear wool on a hundred-degree day?" I exploded. Suddenly Mother grinned.

She was relieved at not having to play out this charade. And as an unspoken token of her approval of my independence she gave me some of her jewelry which I should not have received from her till the day of my marriage.

Father too made a half-hearted attempt to find me a suitable match so he might forestall one that my mother might come up with. But that he never really wanted to face the possibility of my marriage was amply clear from his behavior towards any young men I actually knew. He attributed to them the basest of intentions and treated them in the gruffest manner possible. Perhaps he dreaded losing a child with whom he shared a special bond of sympathy. I alone of the children was not afraid of him, nor did I find his orders and instructions irksome as I did Mother's. In fact I felt special when he asked me to help him with the odd task, like stuffing the school fee envelopes with brand new notes, or when he let me pick the piece of music we would listen to together after the other children were in bed. The privileged closeness I had to his introspective and intellectual self made me immune to Mother's tirades against him. But it also made his absence from home much harder for me to bear.

I was eight when it happened. It was November, the month of Divali with its festive lights and fireworks. We were on vacation from school. For weeks the viciousness of my parents' quarrels had steadily escalated. One morning after a night of unremitting violence on both sides Father left and simply failed to return home. Mother had spent the day tearing through the house weeping and cursing. My anxiety grew as twilight faded into night with no sign of Father. As I herded the children to bed I was overcome by a sudden uncontrollable shaking of my limbs. I knew something awful and irremediable was happening, but I could not fathom its meaning. All night as I lay awake listening to my mother's keening I waited for a familiar footfall on the garden path. It never came. On the advice of his lawyer Father had moved into a friend's home in anticipation of filing for divorce. But no one told us anything, and even Mother was in the dark about his intentions. For three days I did not know where my Father was or what was to become of us. For three days I stood mute and cold, watching my mother's fury and agony. On the fourth morning his solicitor arrived to talk to her. He was a friend of the family. In view of the number and ages of the children he advised her to seek a reconciliation. Finally Mother got dressed in her green chiffon *sari* and drove off with him. I went around and locked all the doors. Then I sat in the middle of the marble floor holding the baby who would not or could not stop crying.

At dusk Mother returned, alone. Then she told us what was happening. Father did not want to be with us any more and wanted a divorce, a term she did not bother to explain. He had moved in with another family and clearly appeared not to miss us. She had seen with her own eyes the huge box of Divali fire-crackers, bigger than any he had ever bought for us, that he had presented to his friend's two sons. She made it clear that our loss was their gain. I couldn't bear to hear any more. I went and hid, and for the first time since he had left I wept with envy and hatred of those two nameless, faceless rivals for my Father's affection. I could just imagine that box full of catherine wheels and sparklers, comets, rockets and fountains. I could just see him helping the boys set them off. Since that day I have never felt the pain of separation from someone adored without the accompanying anguish of a possessive rage.

Father did return eventually, but this was only the first of several such departures and reconciliations. Slowly, painfully we learned of the existence of the other woman. My brother and I had even met her at a lunch in a strange restaurant with walls draped in red velvet and an overpowering smell of *attar.* The place, the person, the encounter all felt somehow wrong. She had seemed so common that we couldn't conceive of her as a rival to our mother or a threat to us. But she was there, a constant presence hovering just off-stage, a danger without a name whose shadow we caught sight of in our mother's eyes. Knowing about her abruptly ended my childhood.

Each time Father failed to come home I felt that numbing nausea and such utter desolation that tears were meaningless. Mother accused me of being uncaring and unfeeling as I sat in a corner with my nose buried in a book. She never understood that my hells have always been private. Nor could she fail to notice that in spite of my sympathy for her I blamed her for his absence. I resented her inability to right things. Every time he returned the bitterness of his betrayal overwhelmed the love she felt for him. She seemed unable to stop herself from driving him further away with her need to make him pay for her pain and humiliation. She did not want to live without him, but she was not ready to let go of her sense of grievance which would have allowed her to keep him. Nor apparently was he able to make the necessary gestures of contrition to soothe her injured pride. I could see that he was in the wrong but did not have the heart to condemn him. I could see she was hurt, but could not fully embrace her crusade against him. And so for many years I walked a thin line between my father's anger and my mother's ravaged self-esteem.

* * *

Now I have chosen to live in America, a land where men do not weep and women do not pray. As I watch the stealthy snow rob the world of its outlines, I think of the fat drops of monsoon rain that beat a tattoo on banana leaves and drip from flower to leaf and fern to moss. The twilight bazaar odors of frying spices, jasmine garlands, and sweat are harder to conjure up with each passing year. Most of all I miss the endless carnival of life lived in the streets: the crowd around the astrologer and his parrot, the carts full of gunny sacks maneuvered through throngs with amazing agility, the rocks on the seashore covered with gaudy miles of the dyer's most recent handiwork, the shocking pink and bilious green of the sweet-seller's wares. Hoping to separate out the skein of myself from the tangled whole of the family, I do without the familiar and the known, away from the demanding love of a brother or the shield of a father's solicitude.

I had a dream recently. I was on a bus full of tourists traveling for endless miles over an immense brown plain with nothing to relieve the monotony of the barren landscape. The earth seemed to heave and sigh in the shimmering heat as we jolted along for hours. Suddenly a ring of mountains rose abruptly into view. A fiery sunset sky formed a backdrop for their dark silhouettes. The road led into the area encircled by the mountains. It held a lush forest with a shallow stream running through it. In the middle of the stream stood a house. It appeared to float on the gently bubbling waters. An open veranda jutted out at one end parting the stream like the prow of a ship. We entered the house and walked through the high rooms. I seemed to recognize the objects and furnishings and felt a satisfaction at their appropriateness there. Through the windows I could see the mountains cradling the land and the house. Leaving the rest I walked quickly out to the veranda. The moment I reached it the house became mine. The lowering sun got caught between two peaks. I heard the water murmur below. I was filled with a deep pleasure at having arrived. There would be no more traveling for me. I politely showed the others out of the front door and turned to take full possession of what had always belonged to me. A perfect tranquility suffused the world. The unexpected sound of my father's voice from somewhere deep in the house made me laugh aloud.

GLOSSARY

Aghori a sect worshiping Shiva; credited with digging up corpses and eating them.

Ahriman primeval source of Evil in Zoroastrianism.

Ahura Mazda the Good Spirit, the supreme Godhead in Zoroastrianism.

Allah the God of Islam.

Apollo Bunder a prominent dock in Bombay, site of the great arch called Gateway of India.

attar perfume made from the oil in rose petals.

bakshish tip, small change given to a beggar.

Bania, Vania Hindu trading castes of Western India.

banyan a huge fig tree (*Ficus bengalensis*) with many aerial roots hanging from it, found throughout India and Burma.

bhajan Hindu devotional song.

Bharat Natyam style of classical North Indian dancing.

bhaya milk-seller, originally from Uttar Pradesh state.

Brahmin a member of the highest Indian castes, traditionally priests.

brain-fever bird hawk-cuckoo (*Cuculus varius*), found throughout India.

burqa long garment covering the entire head and body of Muslim women.

cantonment army encampment, settlement for British troops.

chaprasi doorkeeper, watchman.

Congresswalla supporter of the Congress Party, which ruled India for the first 40 years after Independence.

dagla Parsi man's frock-coat.

dharma duty of any particular Hindu caste.

dhoti man's loincloth.

Divali, Deepavali Hindu New Year.

drongo six species of bird (*Dicrurus* spp.) found throughout India; good mimics.

fenta hat worn by Parsi men.

Ghati primitive inhabitant of the hills.

Goanese native of the territory of Goa, to the south of Maharashtra; usually Catholics, of part-Portuguese ancestry, they are esteemed in Bombay as cooks.

gram chick-peas, parched seed of a vetch (*Cicer arietinum*).

Gujarati person from Gujarat State; also the language of that region.

gymkhana social club where various European sports are played.

hamal doorkeeper, dogsbody.

Hindi dominant Indo-European language of Northern India, and of the film industry.

Jain a religious minority noted for its nonviolence and wealth; followers of the teachings of Mahavira.

karma Fate, destiny.

keffiyeh Middle Eastern headcloth, distinctive of Arab men.

khadi rough homespun cloth, particularly associated with Gandhi's policy of self-reliant home production.

Khoja a Muslim community from Western India.

khokha kind of hat for Parsi men.

koel Indian cuckoo (*Cuculus micropeterus*), a common bird.

kulfi Indian ice-cream.

lagan Gujarati word for "marriage"

Maharastrian, Maratha an inhabitant of the western state of which Bombay is the capital.

Mahatma a great spiritual leader, especially Mahatma Gandhi.

mali gardener.

Maratha Wars three wars fought between the British and the Maratha forces intermittently between 1775 and 1819.

Marathi the main Indo-European language of Maharashtra State.

mehtrani, matranee a female sweeper.

mofussil rural district.

mogra the Arabian jasmine (*Jasminum sambac*), cultivated throughout India and the tropics.

navjot initiation rite for Parsi boys and girls.

pão bread (Portuguese)

papad wafer made of lentil flour.

Parsi, Parsee Zoroastrian inhabitants of Bombay and nearby parts: they arrived in India as refugees from Persia in the 7th and 8th Centuries A.D.; altogether about 80,000 in India today.

peepul, pipal a sacred fig tree (*ficus religiosa*) found throughout Northern India and Burma.

pomfret genus of marine fish (*Stromateus* spp.) which make delectable eating.

pugree headgear worn by men.

Punjabi people from Panjab State; also the language of that area.

raga in Indian music, a melodic entity prescribing a particular set of melodic possibilities.

rupee the standard Indian currency, today equal to an American nickel.

sahib term of address or reference for any European man.

sari fabric worn draped by a woman.

solar topee pith helmet worn by Europeans in the tropics.

Strumwelpeter character in a 19th Cent. German cautionary tale for children.

tandarosti prayer for health and long life.

teak an important Indian and Burmese tree (*Tectona grandis*).

thali brass tray on which a variety of dishes are served together.

zamindar land-owner.

Zoroaster prophet of ancient Persia.

Biographic Note on the Author

W. D. MERCHANT, born in 1946 in Bombay, was educated at Elphinstone College, Bombay University, and then moved to the U.S.A. in 1967 to complete her graduate studies at Western Michigan University and the University of Chicago. The author of several articles, this autobiography is her first book. She now teaches sociology and anthropology at South Suburban College, in South Holland, Illinois. She enjoys off-beat travel, restoring houses, and pampering her Maine Coon cat. Her brother is the poet Hoshang Merchant, author of *Stone to Fruit*, *Yusuf in Memphis*, and *Anaïs Nin: Indiscretions*.